A Ceremony Called Life

WHEN YOUR MORNING COFFEE IS AS SACRED AS HOLY WATER

TEHYA SKY

sounds true
BOULDER, COLORADO

Sounds True
Boulder, CO 80306

This work is solely for personal growth and education. It should not be treated as a substitute for professional assistance, therapeutic activities such as psychotherapy or counseling, or medical advice. In the event of physical or mental distress, please consult with appropriate health professionals. The application of protocols and information in this book is the choice of each reader, who assumes full responsibility for his or her understandings, interpretations, and results. The author and publisher assume no responsibility for the actions or choices of any reader.

Cover design by Rachael Murray
Book design by Beth Skelley

Printed in Canada

Kabir poem on page 9 from *Kabir: Ecstatic Poems* by Robert Bly. Copyright © 2004 Robert Bly. Reprinted by permission of Beacon Press, Boston.

Rumi poem on page 81 from *The Essential Rumi,* translated by Coleman Barks (HarperCollins, New York). Copyright © 1995 Coleman Barks and reprinted with his permission.

Hafiz poem on page 189 from *The Gift: Poems by Hafiz* (Penguin, New York). Copyright © 1999 Daniel Ladinsky and used with his permission.

Library of Congress Cataloging-in-Publication Data

Names: Sky, Tehya, author.
Title: A ceremony called life : when your morning coffee is as sacred as holy water / Tehya Sky.
Description: Boulder, CO : Sounds True, 2016.
Identifiers: LCCN 2015044677 | ISBN 9781622037131 (pbk.)
Subjects: LCSH: Spirituality. | Spiritual life.
Classification: LCC BL624 .S587 2016 | DDC 204—dc23
LC record available at http://lccn.loc.gov/2015044677

Ebook ISBN 978-1-62203-712-4

10 9 8 7 6 5 4 3 2 1

This book is dedicated to life.

I have a lot of things to teach you now, in case we ever meet, concerning the message that was transmitted to me under a pine tree in North Carolina on a cold winter moonlit night. It said that Nothing Ever Happened, so don't worry. It's all like a dream. Everything is ecstasy, inside. We just don't know it because of our thinking-minds. But in our true blissful essence of mind is known that everything is alright forever and forever and forever. Close your eyes let your hands and nerve-ends drop, stop breathing for 3 seconds, listen to the silence inside the illusion of the world, and you will remember the lesson you forgot, which was taught in immense milky ways of cloudy innumerable worlds long ago and not even at all. It is all one vast awakened thing. I call it the golden eternity. It is perfect.

JACK KEROUAC,
in *Kerouac: The Definitive Biography* by Paul Maher Jr.

CONTENTS

INTRODUCTION

We weave in and out of ceremony throughout our entire lives. Between our very own births and deaths, we celebrate rites of passage, we lose loved ones, and perhaps we get married, birth our children, engage in personal rituals, attend support circles, or sit in spiritual ceremonies.

No matter what sort of ceremony we find ourselves in, once we are there, we sense we're in the midst of some sort of tangible meaningfulness and at the feet of a mysterious invitation, and for that, our presence heightens, our hearts begin to open, and we're more likely to recognize our role in creating our lives. Indeed, we weave into these sacred moments when we allow ourselves to drop into this deep space of ceremony, once again engaging with the magic of life and soaking up the profundity we crave so much.

But then we weave *out* of these sacred moments when we mistakenly believe that all of life could ever be anything other than a procession of sacred moments, an inherently divine ceremony. We compartmentalize the spiritual nature of our lives, squashing it into one specific corner, rather than allowing it to course the waters of our whole lives, as it naturally does. We build spirit dams, and because of that, we become dry, tame, disjointed, and we do not feel whole. It is so easy to read self-help books, go to yoga class and workshops, and sing *Om Shanti Om*, but at the end of the day, until we realize all of life as the spiritual practice—until we realize the water we drink is the wine of

God—we don't feel the completion we crave. When we begin to see the altar is all around us—in the rocks, the magic of numbers, the miracle of other people, the sound of crunching leaves beneath our feet, our morning showers—all of life is again meaningful, and each moment carries within it the invitation home.

I was first confronted by the seeming deficiency of the sacred nature of my own life when I was working as an artist manager in the music industry. Since I was a little girl it had been a fantasy of mine to work directly with musicians, and living it out was a dream come true, until it wasn't. At twenty-six, I realized the path I was going down was no longer right for me, and that the longer I remained on it, the more disconnected I felt from my soul and the generous, good nature of life.

I tried to talk myself out of leaving for as long as I could, fearing the end of the secure life I knew so well, but eventually, the call of life was screaming through my soul and was impossible to ignore. *It is time to follow your heart. It is time to resolve the pain, meet your true Self, and learn and live your truth.* So I followed the wild call of my being to a commune in Central America to see what would happen if I let go of who I *thought* I was in favor of finding out who I *truly* was. As crazy as it seemed to leave such a promising career and head to the jungle with no plans and very little money, it was undeniably time to let go and dive into the unknown.

Allowing myself to trust that mysterious guidance and the magical call of life, no matter how unreasonable or insane it sounded, proved to be the beginning of my return to the true nature we all share: that of a wise, intuitive, joyful, free being; part God, part human, home to the true master that lives within; destined to create many good things. Indeed, since walking off the cliff of that secure life and into the free fall of following my energy wherever it takes me, of allowing life to be a meditation, I have remembered to appreciate each step of the journey as just as sacred as the next. I have remembered that every tear and challenge is just as meaningful, benevolent, and welcome as every gust of bliss and surge of joy. I have remembered that our presence and our accountability are the weavers of our best destiny.

I have also remembered that when we keep our attention inward with the stillness, remembering the life we experience to be a reflection of what we hold inside, and work with what we see in that mirror for our freedom, we are empowered, we open more, we move away from fear and into love, and we are able to do our best. And, finally, I've been reminded again and again that our willingness to show up for it all without judgment—our willingness to keep our eyes and hearts open and our awareness sharp—is the current that keeps us harmonized and going wherever we are best off going, continuously delivering us to the sweetest, most fulfilling visions of our lives.

This book is about all of that. It's dedicated to helping you remember how to experience all of life as the precious ceremony it is. It's an invitation to remember how to wake up each morning—whether you're happy or sad, whether you're alone or in the arms of your lover—knowing that you are in a unique ritual and gift of life, and how *that*, in and of itself, is profoundly and inherently *miraculous*. It's about the opportunity you have to stand there while your oil gets changed and be absolutely mystified and amazed or even simply curious about that simple miracle: that you can stand there, that there's a car, that you happen to be doing this, that you are breathing, that you also happen to be passing through an intense breakup or just had another beautiful day. This book is about the opportunity we have to wake up not only through the profound and dazzlingly spectacular moments, but also through the mundane, the challenging, the seemingly meaningless or *please-can't-you-just-end-already* moments that make up the expanse of our lives. Indeed, it's about discovering the miraculous *through* the mundane, the Godself *through* the human self, and the beauty that abounds when we stop denying our humanity and instead integrate the two.

Today, through my work as a metaphysical guide, channel, and writer, I share this way of living and being with others. Whether in personal relationships, work with clients, or work with myself, I rest my focus upon the simplicity and perfection of this moment; the storyless experience and honoring of the feelings within it; what there is to learn, "heal," or align, when needed; and the journey into that which limits us, disempowers us, and keeps us playing small—all of which are insights we explore in this book.

What I share here is a reminder of what we all already know. We just need to be reminded of the essential teachings of life now and then. Why? Because we are on a profound journey of remembering our divinity in a world that still fights against it. Because we are still learning how to be human. Because we have absorbed at least a few layers of conditioning, and for that, it is inevitable that our perspective clouds and clouds again. So many of us are doing our best to remember and align with the power of love, presence, and grace, and it's always helpful to have some outstretched hands to hold along the way. This book is offered to you in this way.

To help us drop into a new understanding and embodiment of our divine nature, we will begin by taking a closer look at what it means to be "spiritual" and what it means to tap into our unconditional spiritual nature. In that discussion, we'll take spirituality off its pedestal and put it onto the seat beside us, where it can giggle with us at the madness and the glory of this life. From there, we'll dive a bit deeper into demystifying the old ideas, concepts, and obstacles that tend to keep us feeling separate from our true nature and the Divine. After that, we'll explore what it means to embody our sacred nature of Creator and Created, and in doing so, we'll talk about how we can truly live life as the spiritual practice that it inherently is. It is my prayer that upon having diffused the confusion about what it means to be human and infused that perspective with the glory it deserves, we will begin to remember our true nature and the gift of our Earthwalk, and we will re-emerge at the end of this book as more awakened, empowered, and ceremonious individuals.

Through this writing, may you come to see that all of life is a ceremony for your awakening, your expansion, your joy, and your love, *when you are present to it.* Something happens in your day—an emotional trigger, an argument, a boring lunch break, amazing sex, unexplainable tears, weirdness, a profound joy, laughter, a breath in, a breath out—and there begins a new moment in the ceremony. You are learning, you are expanding, you are appreciating, you are opening and contracting, only to open again more into love. You are infinitely wiser from your connection to the teachings of the Guru of Life. And what is more worthy of awe, what is more worthwhile, what is more ridiculously and absurdly miraculous than that?

Part One

I AM

Recalibrating Our Vision
of Spirituality

Chapter 1

WHAT IS
SPIRITUALITY?

Are you looking for me? I am in the next seat.
My shoulder is against yours.
You will not find me in stupas, not in Indian shrine
rooms, nor in synagogues, nor in cathedrals:
not in masses, nor kirtans, not in legs winding
around your own neck, nor in eating nothing but vegetables.
When you really look for me, you will see me instantly—
you will find me in the tiniest house of time.
Kabir says: Student, tell me, what is God?
He is the breath inside the breath.

KABIR,
Kabir: Ecstatic Poems, versions by Robert Bly

I have to say this now, for if I don't I will burst: *spirituality includes your humanness.* It includes your weariness and stumbles as much as your reverence and joy, and it includes *Seinfeld* as much as *satsang.* It is perhaps confounding for us all that somewhere along the line, spirituality seemed to begin to exclude the ruffled feathers of our humanity. Maybe it's all the conditioning of control and the patriarchal structures, or maybe it's the Eastern focus on enlightenment and nonduality that did it. But whatever is responsible for the misunderstanding that spirituality only breeds on shiny white marble floors—that spirituality is a compartmentalized area of our lives rather than *all of life itself*—I am sure it did not intend for such an epic mix-up.

Spirituality or anything that is meant to explore the nature of being could never reject or exclude anything that exists—period. In other words, spiritual practice includes and welcomes not just your *ommms*, but also your "*ommm*-my God, I'm about to flip out." For, after all, although the former may be peace, the latter is just the perception of an absence of peace and therefore an invitation into the opening and expansion process that life is all about. Our places of discovery, illumination, and breakthrough are not limited to our temples and our mosques but extend into traffic jams, dirty dishes, and even our trips to the mechanic.

What's happened, though, is we have moved so far away from appreciating the sacred, pervasive nature of our vulnerability—which is truly one of our most essential gifts—and as a result of this rejection have struggled, compartmentalized our lives away, and become deeply dissatisfied. For that, it is time to reclaim *what we know in our bones to be true*. It is time to reclaim the spark in our souls and the expansive holiness of our lives.

It is often our ignorance and our ideas around spirituality that keep us from knowing our wholeness. For example, many of us believe ourselves to be "unspiritual" or not into "that stuff," which in and of itself is a debilitating idea. On the other hand, many of us on a spiritual path quietly hope that spirituality is an end to vulnerability and the ups and downs of life. We believe we are out of the grace of God or not doing good enough or regressing or need to grow faster or whatever our particular strand of rejection is—just because we're human.

To that, I say, it is time for an inner revolution—one that burns away that old paradigm, the idea that who we are *as we are* is not enough and that life "gives us problems," and radically welcomes a new paradigm, that honors the full spectrum of our human vulnerability and the teachings of the Guru of Life. This, I am sure, is the only way to remember the wholeness we once knew so well.

If that wholeness is what spirituality points toward, then I say spiritual practice is the practice of becoming more aware, via the human experience, of the divinity and unity consciousness that is everyone and everything. I also say that wherever there is transcendence, there must also be inclusion. In other words, spirituality is working *with* and *through* the human experience for the expansion of our awareness. Furthermore, I'd say it's the practice of anchoring that awareness in the body, which can also be described as merging and integrating the Godself/spiritual with the human self/material. I refer to that merged wholeness as the *Self*. It's a case of "and": We are both human *and* God. We're feeling both frustrated (or sad or angry) *and* at peace. We are both the spiritual (eternal) *and* the material (ephemeral). We created the material *through* the spiritual, which means the material must be inherently spiritual, and now have the unique and wildly magical opportunity of experiencing our Selves, which is what it's all about. By the power of reflection, life is an experience of our Selves (and ourselves, as the case may be). The two simple things this practice of awareness and integration necessitates are presence and accountability.

This understanding of spirituality implies that all of life is a ceremony simply because it is a procession of sacred moments, and all of those moments inherently contain within them the invitation for you to either become more aware or rest in your beingness as awareness itself, as the one who witnesses all. Every single thing from washing the dishes to mowing the lawn is a spiritual activity simply because it involves *you*—a being of inexplicable cosmic presence—and simply because it is happening. It is a moment available for your totality. It is a moment for you to experience the fullness of life through the incredible spectrum of duality. It is a moment for you to appreciate—really *appreciate*—that life is not about making you happy or meeting your expectations. It is a moment for you to appreciate that *all* moments—the "good" moments, the "bad" moments, every kind of moment—are part of the ceremony. It is a moment for the awareness that you are to juice the experience of this divine unfolding—via your presence, accountability, and vulnerability—for all that it's worth.

Essentially, we're always either in a state of presence and peace or we're in a moment that is experienced as an upset: an interruption from that state of simplicity to reveal that which is unresolved within (that which, therefore, welcomes the feeling of upset). This can only mean that even when it's not "good," it's all, actually, truly good, simply because it's all "grist for the mill of awakening," as Ram Dass says. We're either able to stay present and in peace or enjoyment—or we're not, in all of the various ways we masterfully tend to check out. The point is, when we *do* check out and react, it's always an opportunity to discover and disintegrate the little trapdoors that had been locking out peace and wholeness and had been allowing the unconscious to take over. We will be discussing how to work with these opportunities in-depth throughout the book.

We have heard the echoes of the human-spiritual separation misunderstanding through all areas of our lives—in misguided "good advice" like "control your emotions" and "be cool" and in common collective patterns, like leaving relationships when shit hits the fan and rationalizing or soothing yourself out of what you're feeling. Because so many spiritual conversations are often singularly drenched in this "be calm" vibe, our separatist tendencies are often encouraged. Despite our best efforts to make heart of it all, we see the presentation of holiness at the expense of vulnerability all around us. Indeed, we've had it reaffirmed in our spiritual classes and workshops. The way *into* spirituality is the way *out* of being human: "Just picture yourself floating on a cloud." "*Breaatheee* innnto the anger, and let it go." "The light! The light!" And we've cycled it back every time we've flinched in the presence of another's pain, affirming it again both within each other and within ourselves.

We also see this misunderstanding manifest through projections upon, and portrayals of, our spiritual teachers. When we see only one side or aspect of our teachers, like the God aspect or the happy, joyful teacher, and not the vulnerable human side, we fill in the blank of what we don't see with the idea that they're always that peaceful, joyful, and so on. The absence of displayed vulnerability is often translated into the silent subconscious idea that we, too, should be like that. "By transcending the ups and downs, I, too, will know the peace he or she knows," we begin to believe.

When we degrade, avoid, or try to control our inevitable human changes, energetic fluctuations, and vulnerability, what happens is that rather than moving into peace, we instead split ourselves and strengthen the defensive structures that act as veils to knowing our divine nature. By choosing to view any part of ourselves or our lives as *not sacred*, we only magnify the feeling of separation within us. And, to bring it full circle, the wound of separation is the core issue spirituality helps to resolve.

The sense that we are somehow separate from the whole—whether that whole is other people/love or God, the Divine, the Universe, Source, Truth, Unconditional Love, Great Spirit, All That Is, Creator, or any other term that may resonate for you (to me they all point to the same one essence we all share)—is the root issue we bring awareness to on a daily basis when we become spiritually inspired. *What is it that propels me out of love and wholeness and into this state of aggravation and fear? What is beneath this trigger that can lead me back to wholeness?* This sense of responsibility and willingness to look at what's really going on is *accountability.*

Accountability, as it relates to becoming more aware, is about our choice to trust that we are responsible for the way we see things, and that the way we see things is neither right nor wrong but simply a reflection of our experience. It's about the choice we have to acknowledge that our perspective is often distorted—and to be responsible for that. Accountability, in this sense, is for our entire lives, from what we attract and how we react to what we feel and what we believe. It's about showing up for ourselves and our lives and doing our best.

When we embrace, appreciate, and explore our passing moments, including the challenging moments that crop up in our external lives, our inner worlds, and our relationships, we start moving into the ceremony of life where all is a sacred gift and all is pointing toward our wholeness. In the ceremony called life, *life itself* is recognized as the spiritual practice, and we work with all of it to become more aware, anchor that awareness within our bodies, and move into our integrated Selves. Indeed, we need to be willing to get messy if we're going to pull the weeds from the dirt. We must go *through* the challenging moments and feelings rather than turning around to exit the same way we came in, because to do that would be to cheat ourselves of the gifts and illumination that wait through the tunnels of our inner realms. We must also be open to receiving the beauty that is before us, because it's not always about work (and even when it is, the "work" can certainly include this enjoyment). It's only work when we're not present and okay with what's happening here and now.

When we turn our perspective on its head, we begin to realize that *if every little thing we experience and feel is an invitation to know God and our true Selves more, then isn't that miraculous?* When we drink our coffee with totality and presence, savoring and exploring each sip as we go, then we know God through a cup of coffee. When we're at a restaurant and we hear the waiter drop his tray, then we know God through the sound of crashing plates. And on and on it goes. Profound moments of insight and illumination certainly do offer us magnificent glimpses of the Divine, and yet the glimpses offered by the mundane are equally majestic. And what we see is that all of life is a ceremony where divinity infinitely bursts at the seams. This metaphor creates a nice, fertile ground to approach our daily lives with, that we may receive and work with each moment in a nice and gentle way.

This profound opportunity we have to live from the inside out—to move into holy union by simply working with life as it happens—is profoundly magical, though not unique. It's important to recognize we've all got the same keys to the kingdom inside of us, and no matter who we are, what religion or tradition we do or don't follow, or how many times we have or haven't gone to Burning Man or Mass, each one of us is just as connected and godly as the next. Every single one of us is a child of the Universe; we're all part of the cosmic dance. We've all got this potency, this magic inside—it's what lights up our bodies and pours through us as inspiration. It's the love we feel. It's the dance we dance when we know we are free, the song we sing when we really let go. It's the glimmer of hope, the ray of light we just *know* is there in our hardest moments.

The ceremony of life begins the moment we become aware that we are in a ceremony at all. This is the drawing back of the curtains where all begins to be revealed. Through our presence (which is simply the here-now, silent, eternal essence of our being that's unrelated to any past or future) and accountability, moment by moment, all unravels into the deeper, truer layers, and both the treasures within us and the treasures of existence come to reflect before us like the wild prisms they are.

If we are to allow our life to be the spiritual practice it inherently is—one of expansion, wildness, anchoring, and peace—then we would benefit by considering something I like to call *Divine Perspective*. This is a key term for understanding both the ceremony and our human condition. Consider it like this: you, in your mind, have particular perspectives on various things. I might ask you, "What is your perspective on your urge to leave your job?" And you might say, "Oh, Sky, I am dying to get out of there, but I just don't know how I'll pay my bills. My perspective is that I'm anxious, but that's just me. My dreams are unrealistic. I'm going to stick it out." In this example, your dominant perspective—the way you see the situation and believe it to be—is rooted in the mind's conditioned perspective of security, fear, and self-preservation. When we consider the Divine Perspective, however, we consider how the all-knowing, ever-harmonious, and generously abundant Universe sees things. The Divine Perspective, in this example, might be, "This is your opportunity to move out of fear and into alignment with your true Self. It is time for you to grow and evolve and break through all that holds you back from living a more fulfilling life and loving more. It is safe, and it is time for you to trust. You will be taken care of. Take the leap of faith."

When we merge with the Divine Perspective, we follow the deeper, fearless voice of our intuition and, in doing so, align with that which is best and most fulfilling for us—for, after all, our intuition could only ever be in alignment with the Divine, because it is our own inner divine whisper. You can consider the Divine Perspective as a clear view of what is objectively happening. Why we even care about this perspective at all is because it is the guidance for the integration of our Godself and the human self, which is often a process of releasing the limiting elements as we discover them through various moments of life so that we may clean the mirror of perception and see ourselves, life, and the possibilities more as they truly are—and melt into love. As we move into deeper integration of the two into one through the ceremony of life, we remember more and more how to effortlessly create and live out the sweet visions of our divinity in our human form. When we are in alignment, it is much easier for our presence to anchor and to be receptive to all the love that is everywhere.

As you begin to realize your life for the spiritual practice it is and forfeit your isolated *self's* perspective with the Divine Perspective, you begin to notice the ceremonial nature of life on a more regular basis. Indeed, it is through the eyes of the Divine—which is the soul of your very own eyes—that you notice the unconditional divinity of life and of yourself and see that reflection of divinity in others. When your chair is positioned facing the wall, you see the wall. When it is positioned facing the sea, you see the sea. The same is true for us. The difference between a life of peace and a life of problems is only *perspective*. Perspective is everything, so we must align with the Divine.

The Divine Perspective includes the awareness that we are forever learning and growing. Evolution for evolution's sake inspires the undercurrents of our lives. With that in mind, we know there are certain aspects of our minds, memories, and so on that may distort our perspective, and we remain sharply focused on letting those things come to light so we can learn from them and move on. This is awareness in action. This is accountability in action. And this is *love* in action, too.

So to those of you who consider yourself to be "spiritual," I encourage you to not stop there. If all of life is spiritual, then that identity of being a spiritual person fades away. I also encourage you to consider the parts of yourself you may have stuffed down, ignored, or never visited—the ways in which you've perhaps become overly detached—for fear of interrupting a peace or stability you've perhaps grown comfortable in. As we move forward in our discussion, it will be very helpful to be open to whatever natural experience of inquiry may arise.

To those of you who consider yourself to be unspiritual, I want to remind you that spirituality has nothing to do with seriousness, sacrifices, or strictness, or with any dogmas or beliefs. It also has nothing to do with conspiracy theories, hippies, psychics, or chia seeds. Nor does it have to do with getting rid of your possessions and especially not eliminating your desires. Rather, it has to do with simplicity and truth and the enrichment that follows in its myriad glorious forms: love, intimacy, celebration, freedom, creativity, playfulness, silence, nature, music, enjoyment, and so on. Understand also that the best thing that could happen to you is that you lose yourself, for only by losing yourself can you know your true Self. And true power. And true love. And so on.

To those of you who feel you are already aligned with the vision of spirituality shared here, I encourage you to continue to gently work with life and to go easy on yourself. It's just as important that we put our feet up, eat something naughty, and watch some TV here and there as it is to sit in meditation, eat mindfully, and cultivate inner peace. One of my favorite sayings is "Everything in moderation, especially moderation."

To all of us, I tip my hat to our courage—and remind us that we are all brilliantly *predisposed* to remember this divinity. It is our very nature. It is our heartbeat. It is our breath.

It is us.

Chapter 2

THE GIFT
OF DUALITY

> If we sing the song of consciousness till we feel the burn of truth, we
> throw a burst of fire into the darkness of psyche so we can see what
> we're doing . . . what we're truly doing, not what we wish to think we're
> doing. This is the untangling of one's feelings and the beginning of
> understanding why love and life are to be lived by the bones.
>
> CLARISSA PINKOLA ESTÉS, *Women Who Run with the Wolves*

If we are to work with the different moments of life to become
more aware, then we need to know how we ourselves work. And
if we are to understand how we work and what's going on in this
crazy magic life, then we need to talk about duality.

Duality is the state of existing in two parts. It's that aspect of life
that gives way to opposites and polarities, like happiness and sadness,
up and down, male and female, and pleasure and pain. The two
main aspects of this dimension that we perceive—consciousness
(light) and unconsciousness (darkness)—are dualistic in nature.
Duality is that which inspires the perception of things as existing
separately from one another, a perception that life on Earth is
largely dependent upon. Without the separation we perceive and
experience through duality, we would not be able to distinguish
between me and you or to hug, touch, eat, and so on.

Duality is often bemoaned as the force of the pendulum that drives us from sanity to insanity and everything in between. Although duality is often associated with the challenging aspects of our human condition, it is actually one of the best things that ever happened to us, because it is what makes it even possible for us to experience anything at all. How? First off, the dualistic nature and contrast of emotions, experiences, and so on sensitizes us, enhances our feeling of them, and helps us to know them more. Consider it: How could you know the feeling of freedom without knowing what it feels like to be trapped or stuck? How do you know the quality of white without seeing black? How do you know the preciousness of joy without having experienced the poetry of sadness? Indeed, duality is a lens that allows us to perceive and feel the nuances of life.

Another way in which duality is integral to our human experience is through the intrinsic role it plays in manifestation. Through the perspective of duality, the separation between the experiencer and the experience is born—and creation becomes possible. When something is one, it is simply one. For it to become two, it must split, and one part must move away from the other. When that happens, a space is created, and it is through that very space that our thoughts, visions, prayers, and intentions can travel and manifest in our lives. The condition of duality gives space for the experience to therefore be born, and for the experiencer to witness and direct the creation of his or her life.

Without duality and this human experience, we'd be in that free heaven space all the time, but it would not be Earth. It would not be ice cream or cuddles or sunsets or tears. There would be no savoring of chocolate, no dogs covering you in kisses, no children amazed by the rain, and certainly—most certainly—no mind-blowing sex. Without duality, we would be in that beautiful space of oneness and love all the time, which would be diiiiiivine, but nothing would be happening out of it. In your inner world, nothing needs to be "happening." In your deepest inner world, nothing *is* happening. But in the outer world, for as long as we're on this planet, things quite obviously must happen.

We came here to experience life—*all of life*. And we could only have this experience if we turned off certain things we knew and could perceive, for that limited vision enables us to have the viewpoint and focus needed to experience all of this. Perhaps a helpful analogy is this: when you go underwater to explore the riches of the sea, you have to alter your way of breathing in air so you can remain underwater. So, too, must the free and boundless spirit alter its experience of its natural, omniscient way if it is to function within the human experience.

Although separation is a holy impression, the thing to remember is that it is an *impression* and not a truth; when you look deeper and deeper within each thing that appears in the spectrum of duality, you eventually get to oneness—the same source of origin, which is also often referred to as "unity consciousness." When we talk about unity consciousness, it's my sense that what we're talking about is God. I would describe *unity consciousness, oneness,* and *God* as synonymous terms for the original source of energy of all things and all existence, to which all things are unconditionally connected and eventually return.

In considering the relationship between the indivisible one and all that this oneness contains, I like to consider the sound *om*. If *om* is the sound of oneness, then within that one sound are also barking dogs, dinging cash registers, footsteps, and songs. This is what the lens of duality lets us see. It is a metaphysical game of energy because all of it is always one, but the seemingly separate pieces are the sacred reality of our human lives nonetheless. Forever and ever, whenever we zoom in to that which appears to be separate, what we see is the same original source—the same heartbeat, if you will. It is the undivided consciousness and love that we all share, and it is the source of our very presence.

The Experience Is Not the Experiencer

Duality is a gift, as long as we do not believe that it is what we are. Actually, even when we believe we are it, duality is still a gift, for when that identification happens, it is specifically our perspective that presents the challenge and not duality itself. Indeed, believing ourselves to be the experience—*confusing the experience with the experiencer*—causes much suffering in the world. When we believe ourselves to be that which we experience, whether it is the thoughts that cross our minds or the range of emotions we feel, we become identified. When we become identified with *anything*, we move out of the perspective from which we can know our true, indefinable, constantly transforming being and into the perspective of separation. Furthermore, when we become identified specifically with the experience of duality, we chase our tails all over its spectrum, ricocheting like mad between happiness and sadness and pleasure and pain in our pursuit to obtain an identified understanding of ourselves. We do this because we feel most safe and comfortable in the land of the known: attachment, stories, and definition.

Anything that we can *consciously see* we associate with the light and we interpret as being known, especially if it is defined. At first, we are often more comfortable in that than we are in the mystery of oneness, because whatever we *can't see* we often associate with darkness. There is a great fear of the unknown amongst humankind, but we must remember that *if it exists, it is the magic of the gods*. And if it doesn't exist, well, then there's nothing to worry about.

Duality is not who we are, it's just our 3-D glasses that allow our human experiences to spring to life. It's just what we're experiencing. And every experience needs an experiencer—and that witness, that experiencer—*you!*—is the essence of oneness itself.

Once we're here in human form and go through all the crazy, painful stuff we indeed go through, it's natural to wonder why we would ever willingly put ourselves through this. But indeed, life is a ceremony in which we get to know this wild human experience where the thoughts we believe and the intentions we hold manifest before our very eyes, where we create that which we experience. This is a land of supreme privilege, where we, as individuated creators, may remember our godly heritage and choose to create the conscious desires of our heart. When we root in unity and experience duality from there, we move into that fertile ground where we're able to create great magic in our lives.

Every single thing we manifest exists within the playground of duality—of experience and experiencer—because otherwise, what are we manifesting? We don't need to manifest love because we are love. We don't need to manifest silence because we are silence. Nor peace, because we are also peace. The stuff that is the nature of our being we don't need to manifest; we just need to unearth. Everything else is a passing experience, and it is the glory of a zillion passing experiences that make up the tapestries of our lives.

The Light and the Dark

Often, when we become aware of the original duality of the light and the dark and how it comprises our very being, we do a very human thing and judge the light as "good" and the dark as "bad." Because our human experience and vision are dualistic, we are prone to perpetuate the breaking down of things so that we may understand them, and we define and judge things in that process of narrowing things down. But throughout all of that, the main thing we're all trying to remember is simply that love is safe and that we are safe in the open mystery of all-encompassing oneness. We're trying to remember that we don't need to understand things in order to be safe and that all we need to do to get through it all is accept, sense, and feel our way there.

The belief that the light is good and the dark is bad is where spiritual ambitions and confusions often begin to creep in. We become aware of our darkness, and we want it extinguished by the light. We become aware of the light, and we want it and only it. We mistakenly believe in a life that is both here on Earth (dualistic) and pure light (God)—without darkness. We believe in a life of pure happiness where every day is filled with laughter, relationships are always pure bliss and great sex, and we can eat pizza till the sun comes up without ever feeling ill. Essentially, we want only the "good" parts of the spectrum. We want to cherry-pick life, and when we are rolling like that, there is a denial or a resistance of anything that does not fit into that luscious good vibe. And when we're denying any part of life we are denying our Selves, the remembrance of truth, and the full experience of it all.

Only when we finally drop this nonsense and recognize all of life, the entirety of the spectrum, all of the good times and the hard times, as equally sacred, as equally ceremonious and worthwhile, are we finally in a position to carry on in a deeply meaningful way. Only then does the taste of the sourest lemon throw our writhing head up to the sky to see the sun. For then we are aware of the true benign nature of the darkness and the light, and we are able to work with them in an empowering way that supports our appreciation and growth.

To be sure, just because the darkness and the light are equally sacred does not mean we benefit by becoming complacent about the darkness we may meet in ourselves. Ultimately, if we are to cleanse the mirror of perception and purify ourselves, then we must bring light into the darkness. That's always been the path of consciousness and the movement of illumination. This coexistence of darkness and light indeed creates a dance in which the clarity of light is invited to lead, but it does not create a hierarchy.

There is indisputably a mysterious dance of consciousness we all experience, and the darkness is a part of it. I wouldn't wish a life of darkness upon anyone just as much as I wouldn't wish a life of *not knowing* the darkness upon anyone. Darkness teaches us about depth, mystery, art, possibility, and trust, for starters. So does the light—but the point is, so does the darkness, and the journey through the tunnel of darkness is a rite of passage that most of us go through. In this dualistic experience, meeting the darkness lets us know the invincibility of the light.

The more we explore and the deeper we go, what we come to know about the light is that it is *invincible*. Once we know the invincibility of the light, we know what I like to call the *ultimate light*, which you can liken to the *soul of light*. It is the true nature of light, which is eternal, absolute, and immutable, includes the darkness, and has no opposite. It's the light that experiences the dance of consciousness, which is the dance of itself.

We have the unconditional opportunity to experience all the moments of life—all the moments of darkness and light—from that space of ultimate light. This ultimate light is our very presence; it is what we are made of. I find that when we begin to realize that our presence is this ultimate light, we can begin to actually remember a time or two where we felt peace even in the midst of chaos or a quiet joy even during profound sadness.

As we begin to remember this ultimate light, we become more willing to face the moments of life with the fearlessness we inherently are. In other words, the various moments of life are witnessed with awareness, with a natural orientation and resting in that which transcends the duality of light and dark (and that which also *includes* it), from the space of God where the two merge into just the throb of existence, the very nature of which is cosmic nothingness light. And for this, there is nowhere to go but here, now.

Sound far out? It is, and it isn't, which is what is so cool. It is so totally far out it extends into a vastness absolutely incomprehensible to our waking mind, and it is all within each and every one of us. In fact, it is in each and every atom of our bodies. Every possibility that ever was, that ever will be, every song conceivable, the information and potential for each of these things rests in our very cells.

The steps you make throughout your journey toward the throne of ultimate light are neither right nor wrong. You're never late to God's doorstep. Your heart will always welcome you; how could it do anything else? And that's also the point: realizing you're always welcome home within yourself, which *is* God's welcome. You *yourself* are the dwelling place of God.

Chapter 3

MASTERY AND THE
FALLACY OF PERFECTION

The word enlightenment conjures up the idea of some superhuman
accomplishment, and the ego likes to keep it that way.

ECKHART TOLLE, *The Power of Now*

The idea that mastery is a state of perfection is a potent misconception, and one that many of us have projected onto our beloved, inspirational teachers and friends at some point. When we project the idealized Self onto others, we essentially do it as a way to remember *our* Selves, so that we may step into the mastery we know in our hearts to be true. It is helpful to pop a hole in the balloon of conflated perfection and mastery ideas so that we may illuminate the remembrance we are gleaning and become aware of our true nature.

When we believe that we *may become* or *should become* completely nonreactive and singularly blissful for the rest of our days, we begin to reject our vulnerability. What happens then is that when we slip, our faith in ourselves slides out the door. Indeed, I have noticed plenty of people become very hard on themselves if, after having a nice, solid, clear stack of days or weeks, they feel overwhelmed by feelings or slip into reactivity to the mind. Shame comes up; frustration, sadness, and even self-destructive tendencies arise. I understand this reaction to what is essentially the feeling that we are "stuck in the wheel" or have "fallen out of grace" because I have gone through it, too.

I went through a period where each time I experienced a prolonged span of peace or bliss, I was sure it would last forever. When it didn't, I attached to the feeling of defeat and, in doing so, believed I was doomed to a terrible cycle, which only deepened the space of darkness and of feeling separate. It would pass and again I would melt into peace and wholeness, and I almost lived in a subtle fear of slipping. Again, a slip would come, and with it shame and defeat.

At some point, I shifted into the knowing that the feelings of shame and defeat (aka my emotional reaction to not being able to live up to my distorted perspective of perfection and the ideal Self) were the engulfment itself, and that the shifts and the cycles themselves were a benign, benevolent, and integral part of life. I realized the peace and the light within were completely independent of the changing energy and were always there, watching. That's why I kept expecting them to last forever, feeling the knowing that "but wait, the light and the peace are meant to stay forever" deep in my bones—because they do. Because they *are* forever.

Mastery *includes* our imperfection. Imperfection is often that which keeps us shifting and evolving. Perfection implies conclusion, something that has reached a state in which there is nothing to expand upon. Therefore, being in one's mastery only equates to perfection in the sense that perfection includes imperfection. On this planet, there is no such thing as something that is both alive and completed, with no more expansion possible. Duality ensures this. All that is alive is in a fluid state of evolving and is constantly shifting, changing, and moving toward expansion. That includes us—our consciousness, our clarity, and our expanding and contracting hearts.

Mastery is nothing more than the state of integration of the Self. It's not that when we begin to embody our mastery, we then have nothing more to learn and never have a moment of contraction again. Rather, mastery has to do with the *place* from which we learn, the perspective we embody, and the way in which we receive *ourselves*—the compassion and lightness we share with ourselves. Being in one's mastery indeed may include moments of finding ourselves triggered, moments when there is sadness or anger passing, and so on. The difference though is that as we move into mastery, we stop identifying with the experience. When we realize we are peace itself (which can only ever happen on its own, experientially, and could never be an intellectual knowing), the way in which we interact with the moments of being triggered and moments of challenge changes. There may still be an outright slip of reactivity, but the difference is in the perspective and the way we handle it, how we embody our accountability. Because we know we are the peace behind the experience, we choose to interact with the situation in a way that opens up new room within ourselves for love or to simply watch while the moment passes. There is no formula. Our needs often change on a moment-to-moment basis—the point is that the master within is also the eternal student.

When we are in our mastery, we do not cease to feel. Rather, we are more alive, more touched by life because of our embodiment of openness and acceptance and feeling from the space of detachment/nonidentification. If we are not the experience and are simply witnessing that which is passing, then often we begin to feel the freedom to explore the experience because it becomes less serious. From these expanded experiences, we take what we need and give back the rest. We allow ourselves greater exploration because of our capacity to be gentle with ourselves as we meet the places within us that are still evolving into light, into cleansed perspective. A moment of mastery is one in which we allow and are compassionate with our imperfections; we are *present with* and *accountable for* that which we experience, recognizing it as a reflection of the beauty that we are or as showing us where we can cleanse the mirror and become more aware.

This space of mastery is indeed the most indigenous way of our being. This presence that always lives on is the inextinguishable shine behind every lie we tell ourselves about our smallness, behind every moment we stop believing in the power of love. It is the way of remaining present, relaxed, gentle, and creative, the way of resting in the heart of awareness. It is a definitive choice, an orientation, and a perspective—taken, embodied, and therefore put into action in totality and *lived*.

These descriptions are simply meant to shine a flashlight to and fro within us, so that we may see, recognize, and recall our true nature. As we move into remembering the ultimate light and the peace within, the need for definitions and recognizing ourselves as "in our mastery" or this or that fades away. To simply be as we are is enough. Although some definitions and explanations can be helpful roadmaps, they are also superfluous. We must explore way past them into the realm of the unspeakable.

Illumination, Here and Now

You do not need to meditate for ten years until you have an *aha!* moment and meet the master within (although that is the path for some). Mastery is the God essence within every one of us—alive and embodied. We all have access to this inner realm because we are quite actually *made of it*. Indeed, at all times we have the opportunity to be in the space of transcendental awareness whilst living out our very lives—again, rooting in unity and experiencing duality from there.

You can be in this masterful space of awareness with both your feet firmly planted on the ground whilst simultaneously going about your life. Being connected, one with the God space within, does not equate to disappearing into the stars and losing earthly connection or enjoyment. It certainly is a possibility to meet illumination in that way, but it does not need to be like that. Rather, we may choose to practice the grounding out and anchoring of our presence into our bodies on a day-to-day basis through all that we do. After all, we are beings of this planet, and we are meant to be here, on this plane of existence (for now, at least).

Do you notice by now how onboard life seems to be with your enjoyment of it? Life wants you to ravish it, to pull it by the hair. Life wants you to make her your mistress. Life wants you to climb in, get onboard, stop worrying so much and taking it all so seriously, and just let yourself be free.

Awake in the Dream

Do we reach a pinnacle of self-realization and remain forever in bliss, smiling, never touched by anything other than the clear light of God? Over and over again, the answer to this is *no*. For most of us, this space of singular unification with the ultimate light is where we go when we are dead, out of human form, and no longer alive on this planet. While alive, we are still needed here—grounded and integrated on Earth—for in many ways we are each needed for the overall awakening of mass consciousness. That may sound lofty, and my sense is that although it is not the *meaning of life* or the point of our existence, it is still important to recognize that we do affect one another positively as we become more aware. Like lights on a grid, the more and more each one of us lights up, the more and more the other lights switch on as a natural consequence of the energetic influence of the collective. Indeed, we are meant to interact, share, and connect with one another. We are meant to naturally inspire one another by sharing our gifts, our expression, our truths, and our peace.

Life is gorgeous playfulness, a rich kaleidoscope of moments one after the other, each one dissolving with newness's infinite arrival. To play with life through the perspective of the divine witness, to become awareness itself, creativity itself, and freedom itself, over and over again through moments of vulnerability and presence, that's where it's at. When we start to see the poetry of how the light dances with the dark—*that shadow play*—we notice the miraculously tiny bugs, the dust that shines like gold beneath the rocks, the way the wilted corners of the flower fade. The whole world becomes something different. It becomes fully alive for the first time. And that—that's what it's all about. Nothing more and nothing less. That moment of mastery is mastery itself.

Chapter 4

"I AM" AND THE
PROMISE OF YOUR SELF

Nature loves courage. . . . You make the commitment, and
nature will respond to that commitment by removing
impossible obstacles. Dream the impossible dream and the
world will not grind you under. It will lift you up. This is the
trick. This is what all these teachers and philosophers who
really counted, who really touched the alchemical gold, this
is what they understood. This is the shamanic dance in the
waterfall. This is how magic is done. It's done by hurling
yourself into the abyss and discovering that it's a feather bed.

TERENCE MCKENNA,
"Unfolding the Stone," talk given June 1, 1991, in Los Angeles

What response comes when you ask yourself who you are? Are
you a parent, a hard worker, a person who believes in putting
others before yourself? A "good person"? A loving son? Are you
a priestess who has remembered her past lives of being a magical healer in divine feminine form? A yogini goddess? A drug
addict? Depressed? Successful? Happy? Gay? Straight? Are you
just so committed to love and awakening that you feel compelled to point out to all your family and friends just where
they're going wrong?

Look inside. Are you defining or attempting to know and understand yourself through the roles you play; your emotions, patterns, and beliefs; your preferences; your credentials; your job, ambitions, and dreams; or your significant past experiences? Notice it. This noticing is a flashlight illuminating that which disconnects you from the deeper truth of who you truly are. The truth of who you are could never be captured in words. You are not who you think you are. If you think it, you're not it. Keep traveling deeper into the inquiry. The mind has no place in the sentient exploration of Self.

If words have arrived, it means the mind has processed the feelings, the realizations, through the filters of conditions, patterns, religion, beliefs, and so on. It is like processed food. You are taking that nutrient-rich, organic smoothie you love so much and pouring it through a strainer and into the little cookie cutter shapes of the subconscious. The seeds are in the strainer—that which is pure is wordless, unutterable. The trick is to just stay with the feelings. You may later point with the great wand of words to the truth you feel. You may also receive divine guidance, insight, and inspiration in the form of words. But that is something else entirely. What we're talking about here are the words tied to identification, analysis, narration, description, and so on, the words that parse, eschew, and mask your sense of your eternal, transcendental nature—your only true heritage.

When you turn inward and ask the existential question *who am I?* to your core of cores, it will never be answered by the mind. The mind may offer up words in response, but it is only telling you the layers above the real answer. The real answer is not even an answer; it is an *opening* that rests quietly beneath the identifications, the intellectual knowing of your divinity, and even deeper, beneath the repressed pain that at some point you decided was *you*. Whatever your story is, the opening is beneath it. It's there as a cellular feeling, a knowingness only truly touched once the previous layers have been penetrated.

We are not the roles we play. The true expression of Mother is not in playing the role of mother and then moving into the role of friend once the kids are gone. The essence of the Mother is a natural current of the feminine and is always present, whether dormant or manifest. It is not necessarily always the primary current, but it is always there. Playing a role, *acting* as Mother is not truly *being* Mother. That is not the current; it is just a script. And the kids will know the difference, just like the lover will know if you are not truly present when making love. Everything is lovemaking; everything has within it this level of intimacy. Being a mother, being a friend, *being* anything, comes from a deep intimacy with oneself. It comes from being one with it, from a willingness to move beyond roles and into the truth of our Self.

To connect with the truth of who we are, we must let go of who we believe ourselves to be. We must be willing to lose ourselves and let the false parts of us die—we must be willing to truly dissolve. Only by losing our self (the identified "I") will we find our true Self. This is what the Sufis meant when they said you need die before you truly live.

Everything in this intuitive-feeling space of remembering the truth within must be approached sentiently, not intellectually. The more we hold on to who we believe ourselves to be, the more we remain in an egoic state and the more we isolate ourselves from truth. Identification is a form of separation; it draws a line between *this* and *that*, and between *me* and *God*. The riddle, the cosmic joke, is that through this "I" we've often felt trapped in along the way, we actually realize the true I. We realize the divine mirror.

Going through the fear of "who will I be if I'm not who I am?" is totally normal, and it's all hype. You're not going to become an extremist who sets up camp outside the supermarket, handing out flyers about God, and become totally unrelatable. It's just not going to happen. Truth, including the truth of who you are, is always simple and never dramatic. It's also unlikely you will decide to live out of a backpack and join an ashram, or that you're going to choose to give up all of your possessions and move into the high mountains of Tibet to be a monk, for that is a dharma enjoyed by few.

When you're ready to let go, you will. Although the deepest truth is that we're always ready, sometimes we still hold on. So until that moment comes, just go easy and remain aware—aware of the fear, feeling the fear—until your surrender travels into transformation.

You see, it's very easy to get attached to the highs of life and be afraid to move into something mysterious, something other than the spectrum of duality you know so well. But if you want to evolve and grow and essentially be alive, eventually you're going to have to let it happen. At some point you will notice the power of surrender, and you'll start to allow it more and more. After your first taste of this resting in the heart, of knowing something beyond "you," you will see how good it is and how nothing is a better high than the ultimate high of truth, which is not even a high and is always there.

When we start to draw back the curtains of the drama created by the attachment to and identification with the mind, we start to see what's behind the scenes. We start to see what's within us beyond dualities. We start to meet the resident master within. And we realize that behind our experience is a being that watches; there is a noticing of the experience. And that noticing, that awareness, is us. As this awareness, we are neither happy nor sad, but simply, unconditionally content. We just are. And we'll see this reflection of our hearts, and we will just fall in love.

Through going more deeply into the truth of who we are, we move into that ultimate throne of awareness. We realize how comfortable that chair is, and we start to choose it more and more. When we realize we're out, we hop back in. And when we realize we're out again, again we hop back in. We get cozy in the meditation cushion of life, and we realize that letting life be as simple as it is reveals to us a formerly unimaginable profundity.

We realize that to let life be the meditation, to simply accept what is and let the truth within us shine, far surpasses both the surge of transient happiness we experience from any pleasure and the stimulation of our various human dramas. We connect with something within us that is divine and true and never changes, that remains while everything outside passes. We start to get to the real stuff, the real God bliss. And the choices we make start to change.

For starters, we begin to choose to stop pretending we *can't* make the choice—the choice of choosing peace over the perspective of problems. We realize that life, raw and wild as it is, is both kind and enough. We begin to stop pretending to be a victim and instead flex our power to choose where we place our energy and, therefore, that which we create and experience. We cease to be the sum of our circumstances, recognizing our perception of that which happens outside of us as a reflection of that which is within. The truth of who we are dissolves the illusions when they arise, simply by our not buying into them and interacting with them anymore, by our realizing they were counterfeit bliss. By and by, oneness dissolves what was once separation.

Jesus said, "I am the Way, the Truth, and the Life. No one comes to the Father except through me" (John 14:6). I'm going to do something brave here and translate what I sense he meant, what his message was when he said that. He means the "I" here is you and that the "me" here is also you. It is a subtle way to trigger you into realizing your true nature. Through your self, you meet God, and you meet your true Self.

This space of godliness—of love—is the common denominator we all share and the space from which we all connect underneath it all. When you start to rest in this space (which takes dedication, so that your energy system can restructure), you notice everything in your life transforms with you. Resting in this space more and more is just an untraining of your energy, a deconditioning so that it may fall into its natural place.

The Witness of It All

I would describe meditation as a practice of deepening one's awareness. The more aware we are, the more we are able to distinguish what's what on the subtle levels, like sensing the moment reactivity comes and choosing to remain present instead. To have our senses fine-tuned is a way of sensitizing our stethoscope through which we sense, listen to, and observe our worlds, so that we may navigate through life with more clarity, power, and intention. The more we rest in a meditative state, the more we realize that life itself is the meditation, that life itself is the spiritual practice.

Now, let's consider a common practice of meditation so we can relate it back to life. When you meditate, you sit and remain present. You relax more and more deeply—and more deeply yet—and remain still. You may find that you become totally unmoving inside—or not. The point is that the focus is upon stillness, even the stillness within the breath. You passively merge with the silence, allowing whatever is passing to pass like clouds. If there are thoughts coming, you let them pass. If there is pain coming, you let it come. You let it move. Whatsoever happens, you just let happen. You allow yourself to just exist and relax, doing nothing, remaining aware *as* the awareness that notices the impermanence of all phenomena.

In between the passing of things, there is a gap. The very existence of this space—simply that *there can be space* between you and that which you witness—reveals the distinction between that which you are and that which you observe. You are that which is inseparable from you—*the witness*, graceful awareness itself. That which watches all, unchanging, unconditionally one with all that is. This is the process of meditation, for which there is no process. This is the process of life, for which there are simply passing moments.

You see, this is why we need to quit placing spirituality on a pedestal and stop treating it like a special realm, activity, or hobby—and likewise stop regarding the rest of life with any less honor than we do "that which is sacred." All that you need is right under your nose, no matter where you are or what you're up to. All of life is spiritual, and every moment is an opportunity to become more aware and know your true Self. Through every conversation, every irritation, every pleasure, a witnessing of it all is the only thing that remains as all rises, climaxes, plateaus, descends, and eventually moves out of existence. You are the observer of the cycles, and your power rests in the space of nonreactivity, in watching and feeling that which happens from the stillness of your being.

I Am

So we realize the great missile of "I am" is not who we *think* we are. Rather, it is the deepest core of knowing within us—the knowing of consciousness, the knowing of the ultimate light, the knowing that lives on. The "I am" is the coming together of the mirrors, the *I* reflecting back on the am-ness until they dissolve back into unity. The I, the Godself, and the *am*, the human expression. God alone is just *I*, oneness, no doing. *Am* is made of two letters and represents the duality of embodiment and action, which can only spring forth out of the oneness. "I am" is the merged Self, the oneness that transcends separation but includes it, feet planted in the earth plane as the master of his or her life, utilizing and appreciating duality as a master tool for creation, and recognizing and seeing love as all.

In other words, it's the realizing that this great space of stillness, of peace, of love is not just God—it's you. You are the awareness that notices the awareness. You are simply this divine beingness itself. And there's no "you" in that. It's not personal. Here, nothing follows the "I am" but the silent, light-filled current of life. You simply *are*—formless and free.

Chapter 5

FROM TRUTH SEEKER
TO CHANNEL

"When someone is seeking," said Siddhartha, "then it happens
quite easily that he only sees the thing that he is seeking;
that he is unable to find anything, unable to absorb anything,
because he is only thinking of the thing he is seeking, because
he has a goal, because he is obsessed with his goal. Seeking
means: to have a goal; but finding means: to be free, to be
receptive, to have no goal. You, O worthy one, are perhaps
indeed a seeker, for in striving towards your goal, you do not
see many things that are under your nose."

HERMANN HESSE,
Siddhartha (Hilda Rosner, translator)

We can seek a job or an apartment and secure it. We can search
for a missing cat and find her in a tree. We can even look for
our misplaced keys and find them just where we left them. The
reason we can locate these things is that, in reality, they exist
outside of us and are separate from our beings. In many ways,
we have a relatively materialistic experience of discovery, but
that process of search and find has no application in the discovery
of truth and the true Self. That which is our very essence can
never be found, only remembered.

"Truth seeking" is a paradox. It's a hide and seek, but truth is not hiding. You cannot capture or obtain truth. The truth is within you, *is* you, and the true you cannot search for yourself. Truth searching for truth? That is confusing. A lost sock looking for itself has only forgotten itself.

We cannot seek that which we already are; we can only allow for it to be remembered and realized through the simplicity of being. The truth seeker is a paradigm, and while the experience of seeking has its place for many of us on a spiritual path, at a certain point it serves us to move out of this paradigm and let it dissolve. We need no paradigm to know ourselves.

Another aspect of truth seeking is one that is often a very well-camouflaged box: *perpetual processing*. Chasing the tail. Spiritually analyzing. Spiraling through the possibilities of duality. Spending years healing wound after wound. There is no end to this process; the spiral is infinite, and the rabbit hole is, too. Keep looking for something to fix and it will be found. But we are not puzzles with pieces hidden in the pyramids. The truth is not complicated; it's not encrypted in our wounds. It is resting in our souls, waiting for the gentleness of our attention.

Often, the inspiration to continue that endless process of healing is rooted in a dysfunction between self-acceptance and perfection. Notice it: Are you waiting to feel you are closer to perfect—that "this is better" or "that is better" in your life—before you can accept yourself? You do not need to wait for your perfection before accepting yourself. There is no redemption in chasing shadows. Besides, the idea of perfection is flawed in and of itself, as we have discussed.

As far as I can sense, the universe is in an infinite, unending creative state. We often call this creative experience *evolution*, and that evolution includes expansion, contraction, movement, creation, death, rebirth, and more. The takeaway here is that, for as long as we are alive, the universe continues to evolve. If the universe were to stop evolving, then it would also stop vibrating and moving, and then everything would stop. Life would cease to exist, because the state of being alive and manifest is dependent upon things vibrating, moving, and *evolving*. As manifest human beings, we are inherently the same. We are the microcosm of the macrocosm, the subjective of the objective. We are always growing, shifting, changing, and evolving. This is the flow of life and what keeps life going.

Acceptance does not mean finality. Check in with yourself: Could it be that you are afraid to accept yourself because once you do, then what? Then you stop growing? It's not that you can only accept yourself once you are perfect, and then that is it. Then you've done it. If it resonates, notice how your lack of acceptance has actually been motivating you to grow. Allowing yourself to be motivated to improve based on the idea that you aren't quite there yet is a collective condition, the presence of which most of us can see in our lives. (Hello—education system, credentials, weight loss, body image.)

The image or idea of a more whole, more perfect me is a common motivation. It's that typical put-a-photo-of-a-skinny-model-on-the-fridge-to-inspire-me-to-eat-well thing. But we do not need to compare ourselves, feel incomplete, or feel inadequate—as if we are not enough *as we are*—to actually grow. We will always grow regardless, even when we believe we are in an amazing space and cannot imagine life getting any better (or any worse, as the case may be). Most likely, we will also contract again even as we embody the incredible wisdom within, because the dance of life is often like that.

We have the natural ability to source our inspiration in the simplicity and the joy of life and of being, rather than in any motivation based upon self-improvement. We do not need to wait until we are "healed" enough before we can accept ourselves.

It's not that our spiritual teachers and leaders don't ever have moments of feeling dislodged from the silence within or painfully aware of the predicament of it all. It's not that they don't have moments of human folly, whether that be in the form of raising their voice at a loved one, getting snappy with a telemarketer, feeling triggered or "off," or simply moments of not being completely present. Whatever their story is, whatever is unresolved or unsettled within them, stumbling can happen. Spirituality *includes* that, and our mastery does too, because it's all about catching ourselves. Every one of us, so long as we are *alive*, is evolving. The key is choosing to evolve with accountability and presence, awareness and compassion. To gently cleanse the mirror of perception again and again.

When we recognize that a lack of acceptance has played a pivotal role in our growth, that it has essentially *inspired* us to grow, we can begin to have an easier time reconciling it. The gift of realizing that *we were only ever trying to help ourselves* is that we can choose to learn in new ways, and we can choose to shift out of that paradigm and into a new one: that is, radical self-acceptance, no matter where we are along the journey, and compassion toward ourselves throughout the ride.

None of this is meant to downplay the significance of trauma, disease, and other distressing life events. Anything that is holding you back or keeping pain within you needs to be brought into the light. But indulging in and romanticizing "processing" leads to missing life by treating it like a process. Every moment energy is shifting and changing. You can dramatize the shifting as a process, or you can liberate yourself by realizing *that's just life*, by letting the fluctuating nature of feeling show you what it needs to on a moment-to-moment basis, without analysis. There is no benefit in attaching a story or an explanation to everything you feel, yet it is crucial to be present and accountable for yourself and your perceptions. Discerning what is worth delving into and what is best to let go of is a subtle art of awareness, and an art that evolves through the practice of meditation.

The truth seeker in you is looking only for you—and for your acceptance. And acceptance is nothing but a total lack of resistance. You are just yearning to live an empowered life of love, simple as that. So let's just keep it like that. Let's move it out of the web of healing and processing and trying to understand and move it into the light of being.

If what we're awakening is the embodied, integrated, Creator-and-Created life of the true Self, then one of the most important starting points is honoring what we feel, including what we feel we *need* and where we feel *to be*. For example, it is possible and supportive to honor your feelings of needing solitude by canceling your evening plans, and even better if you accept your feelings without interrogating yourself, explaining *why*, or creating a story around the moment. When you are honoring your inner guidance and feelings like this, then you're supporting the unfolding of the true way of your life, which is always guided by your intuition (never by logic), and is always taking you home.

The reminder continues to pour in that *whatever feels right for you* is fine. There is no judgment in the zone of real. When you're showing up for what feels right, you are naturally falling into divine alignment, and as a consequence, truth will reveal itself more and more to you. (By the way, "showing up for what feels right to you" just means you are consciously following your intuition, your inner sense of what you need, and where your energy is taking you on a moment-to-moment basis.) Then you're on a clearer path of life as the spiritual practice and honoring the ever-changing moments of your ceremony. Then you're in a powerful flow that pulls you into connection, into the rhythm of the soul. And in that song, each wave pulls you more and more into your inner God-home of wholeness and peace.

Relaxing into Receptivity

Our eternal nature can only *be*. Searching energizes the place from which the searching originates, which is the mind, the exact place we are looking to migrate our energy away from so that it may return to the intuitive heart and body. Indeed, only the mind can seek, and it will never meet the remembrance and inner knowing for which it is seeking. Consider it like this: The seeking mind can only exist on radio channel 17. Truth is within radio channel 0. Only feeling and consciousness can enter channel 0 to meet truth. So seek as you might, your mind will never enter that sentient channel of truth.

On the journey toward truth through channel 0, we can only relax as the stillness *behind* the emotional and mental madness and be open to that which is revealed. That includes relaxing through moments of constriction, fear, and pain and dropping into the presence that notices those feelings. It's not that those things can't appear along the way, it's just that we don't give our power to them via our energy and focus. We don't attach to them or identify with them. We don't tighten and tense, we don't clench our teeth at their arrival, and we neither dramatize nor reject the situation. Rather, we welcome them, giving them space to do their thing, share their wisdom, reveal their golden ticket, and pass. We trust in their presence, knowing that, at worst, they could only ever be a distorted form of love, and therefore rather than indulging or dismissing them, we instead listen for their teaching with the placid temperament of a respectful student. And we refocus, and we reorient. We keep coming back to that dropping into and relaxing into the eternal flame of our presence. And we grow through the meeting, again and again.

By and by, what we realize is that the inspiration and energy that fuels us as channels is the real energy—the raw, pure stuff. The mental energy is a stimulant that makes us crash. We realize that, yes, we *can* rest in our hearts while that which comes through us *perpetually arrives* without force, without role playing, arriving simply with the pure natural breeze of being. This authenticity is magnetic. You can see it in the eyes. It cannot be faked. We are turned on, and it lights up those around us. We're giving back to the world and to ourselves at the same time.

An electric simplicity has arrived.

The Channel

Our truest, highest embodiment is always the most simple. Rather than passionately opinionated individuals on a mission, in our truest embodiments, we are open, receptive, activated channels, gently and strongly expressing the truth we have come to know. Rather than creatures put here to resolve infinite karmic debts and perpetuate the spinning wheel, we are free beings, at our best when we are creating our lives in accordance with our truest will.

It is not that only psychics and mediums are channels. It has perhaps been misunderstood that a channel relays divine information strictly through the translation of messages. However, we are in our receptive channel state when we allow the Divine to course through us and then express that vision, inspiration, wisdom, or movement. We are all, by default, channels.

That pure transmission can be expressed in the form of a poem, a song, a flower arrangement, or even the way we move our body. It can be expressed in the form of realizing mathematical equations, building a table, caring for animals, or making the most delicious muffins. Indeed, it is the Divine's very nature to explore and express itself through *everything*. There is truly no limit to the ways the Divine explores itself, and we are all channels of that divine expression. Every single one of us is made of divine vision and destined to create those visions.

A balanced, activated channel is someone who is totally their true Self. It is someone who explores the gift of the unique Self and shares the expression of their genius in whatever its form. It is someone who takes none of this specialness personally and, in doing so, embodies more and more of their Self. It is one who stays out of the way and lets that which is coming through come through. It is one who breaks through the conditioning of "But I have to be a lawyer or what will happen to my life?" or "It's unrealistic to pursue my dream of being a musician—I'll end up broke!" They let themselves confront that breaking down, that deconditioning, that entering into mystery, on the chance that they may be dazzled by existence; on the chance that their own divinity might make them truly joyful and fulfilled for the first time.

It is only the mind that says the channel has to be something socially and culturally accepted or recognized as awesome, groundbreaking, or legendary for it to be truly adequate or significant. It is only the mind that engages in this false disparity between what is sacred and what is not. You've heard it before: Two people reference the same recipe to bake a cake. Yet one cake comes out mediocre, bland at best, while the other comes out as the tastiest thing to ever grace your mouth. This is because the person whose cake came out delicious allowed love—God—to pour through him while creating the cake, while the other person just followed a recipe (and perhaps thought about the news whilst stirring the batter). It's because the person with the yummy cake, in a whimsy of inspiration, added a dash of chili and a hint of lime—"I know it sounds crazy, but I really feel like throwing it in!"—disregarding the directions and what's been proven to work. That which comes through the channel will always taste a bit different. There's always a hint of the unexplainable.

And that's just what we're ready for in this moment—it's what we're been preparing for all our lives. The truth seeker was a bona fide trick, and now we're just saying, "Hey, I desire to be the master of my life. I'm ready for that. The fire of my being is stoked toward this. All else will burn. I'm ready to take my power back, let God pour through me, and relax. I'm ready for this accountability." We're getting somewhere, and we're simplifying.

Let It Flow

Opening up to the potential of our lives requires us to stop taking ourselves so seriously and so personally. Our lives are not personal. Does that sound crazy? Realize it like this: Only the egoic/identity-based life is personal. The life of the channel is not personal. The life of the mind and ego is identity. It's highly personal, and that is what keeps it so limited and unfulfilling. No matter how much you have or how accomplished you consider yourself to be, the soul longs for the true freedom, expansion, love, and creativity that rests beyond identification—until it finally meets it.

The life of the channel is an opening to God, an invitation for the Divine to pour through as guidance and inspiration in all moments. It's saying, "Hey, I'm a conduit for divine expression. Come through me. Let's do this!" And it's impossible for the divine energy that comes through to be personal. Why? Because divine energy—the energy of God—is always one with everything that exists. It is totally pervasive, unconditional, and inclusive of all. That which is personal is, by nature, conditional, because it is available to some but not to all. Therefore, contrary to what most of us have grown up believing, that which is personal is actually rooted in separation consciousness, and true intimacy—which could only ever be oneness—is rooted in the impersonal love of the Divine. So the highest forms of connection can never be personal. And what's so amazing is that through the opening and tuning in to this impersonal nature of love and divinity, life often becomes truly spontaneous and inspired for the first time.

Spontaneity comes, and you trust it, you go with it, you become it, and this trusting and following life's calls reveals unimaginable gifts to you. You are one with life itself, and so how could you not trust the moment-to-moment inspirations and changes that come? The inspiration comes, and you let it dance through you. When you no longer allow your mind to stop you, what can be created through you reveals its glory and height.

These moments of powerful embodiment and love that you crave in your soul are actually just what you are, albeit through the shifting kaleidoscope of form. You are a vehicle for all of that sweetness, all that playfulness, the watching of life through its infinite shifts, morphs, and changes. We are here to allow the highest truth to pass through us as gorgeous, radiant expression, unique to each one of us—and when we feel like we can't, to be gentle with ourselves. Being yourself is the most natural thing in the world, and yet, in true form to the paradox of life, it is often the hardest thing.

The shades must be drawn back for the light to come through. There must be a willingness to open. That is the prerequisite for this transformation. When the frequency of your desire is stronger than the shackles, the shackles will break. So firstly, you *must*, with *all of your being*, all of your conviction and devotion, your totality and your absoluteness, desire this transformation. From there, the right actions will always follow, and here, "right" means that which is the best next step for you, that which pulls you deeper into alignment, harmony, openness, and truth. That which pulls you into God.

We are each a perfect, unique instrument in the grand symphony of life. Without any one of us, the whole song of life changes. It changes in a very subtle way, but indeed it changes. Imagine life as one big song. If even the most quiet string or chord is not played, the song changes. We are like those quiet strings or chords that together comprise an enormous harmony.

Too many people walk this planet believing they are unimportant, that they *don't matter*. Perhaps you are one of them. However, nothing could be further from the truth. You, *the real you*, is always needed. What isn't needed is the problem paradigm, the suffering, the limiting beliefs, the stories. The ideas about who you are. What *is* needed is your acceptance, your resplendent divinity, your truth, your vulnerability, and your authentic expression—whatever it may be. You being in your flow helps the rest of us fall into ours.

Purifying the Channel

So, if we're going to make the move from being a truth seeker to living the empowered life of a channel, then we need to venture deep within with our sturdiest of flashlights. We need to recognize what we've been up against all these years, shine the light on it, and make the full-power decision to move through it—through all the darkness of beliefs, conditioning, judgments, and repressions—and into the light of acceptance, releasing, opening, and letting go. This is the way to Self-discovery. This is the way to experience the potential of your being, of your life, and of your gorgeous, open heart.

This is not to suggest that you need to delve into your subconscious just for the sake of it. For sure, we can dive deep when we are called to without plunging into unnecessary realms (like over processing, seeking, or self-improving). What we're talking about here is the call to dig deeper when "things come up," like when you find yourself contracting, reacting, triggered, or motivated by fear. This exploration is for those moments and any other moments where you get the sense that you're being limited by your perspective or story.

Just realizing that our subconscious has been imprinted with anything at all is a beginning. We must be patient and loving with ourselves through the journey of opening. In many ways we are like children who were never allowed to be ourselves. We need to go back to the heart of our inner child and free it, so we can finally be allowed to be creative unlimitedly, all over our life, and let our wild and playful spirit run free. That is the heart of freedom. It is with our inner child.

Yes, the breaking down of the barriers—the conditioning and mental structures that limit you—can be intense. Earth rattling. Volcanic. It is actually a deconstruction of your foundation, and it may truly feel like just that. It is a deconstruction of what *seemed* to have been. And it is the only way, this way of purifying yourself and retraining the mind by breaking down the stale, limiting structures that prevent you from resting in love and expanding. You have to get in to see what roots have been temporarily poisoned. Your love will set it all right.

Again, this undoing will happen naturally, as you will continue to be triggered by that which you need to grow through. So I just say it one more time to make sure we are very clear here: this is nothing for you to stage or force or push yourself too hard through. Through the mirror of perception you will continue to see yourself in that which is before you.

You may need to shed a few tears and let some old pain and memories move out of you. Ultimately, as they move out of you, more and more space within will open up. And this open, free space is the space through which your true energy will flow. You will be unclogging the channel. When we go through the gates of this empowerment we enter the furnace of truth. When we are truly ready to let go, the illusions will rise to burn. Through the great stare of awareness all illusions that rise eventually catch fire. The smoke of this fire can feel like confusion as our view is temporarily hazed. This is part of the process of purification. Confusion is not to be feared.

Even amid the burlesque of chaos, the invisible fleck of God will always shine and reflect. *This is the promise of life.* The great stare of awareness will always recognize it, and it will always eventually catch that prism, no matter how infinitesimal it may seem within the scene of the moment. Over and over again, to catch that prism is to lock eyes with the magnetic pull home. We will always sense that magnetic draw, the unmistakable scent of our immortal footpath—upon a journey that no one can walk *for* us or even *with* us, in the truest sense. This is a journey that we can only make alone.

Part Two

MISUNDERSTANDINGS AND DEMYSTIFICATION

Moving Through the Obstacles
That Keep Us Feeling Separate

Chapter 6

MAKING FRIENDS
WITH THE EGO AND MIND

The key to our transformation is simply this: the better we know
ourselves, the better equipped we will be to make our choices wisely.

GREGG BRADEN, *The Turning Point*

The mind has gotten a pretty bad rap over the years. The ego
perhaps even worse. But neither the ego nor the mind can
be held accountable for the fact that they have gotten so out
of control. They are like children who no one knew how to
handle, and so they were left undisciplined. Now their disruptive behavior sets the tone of the entire household.

The issue is not the "problematic" mind or ego. Unlike children, who truly are chock-full of their own soul power, the mind
and the ego have only the power we give them. They are completely responsive to our will, and without our gift of attention,
they are powerless. While they may feel plenty powerful, they
can't actually get their juice flowing without our participation.
Because of their dependency on our direction, the mind and
ego are not the problem so many of us have decided them to be.

No mistakes were made when we were created. We are a quantum essence of energy, mathematics, vibration, and sound—a
gorgeous symphony—and no part of our composition, no part

of our geometric structure, needs to go. Perhaps a few notes are out of key, sure, but there are no design flaws. When the Divine is embraced, all that is created by the Divine is also embraced, because they are one and the same. Nothing needs to be changed or healed within us other than our perspective.

What's the perspective that needs to shift? Ours: That anything, ever, could be a problem. That we shouldn't be the way we are. That things, including us, are not okay as they are right here, right now. As this perspective relates to the ego and mind, there is a collective perspective that's entirely problem-based and draped in story. It is a story told to us by our mind, and it comes from the collective mind. It is a spiritual drama, and in it, we—ourselves—believe *the idea* that we have two enemies: the nefarious dictator, called the ego, and the out-of-control mind that won't stop pushing its agenda. The insane thing is that it is the mind itself that presents this idea. When this story motivates us, we fall into ideas about overthrowing the mind and the ego so that we may finally live from the heart (a romantic ending!), but it's all just the confection of the mind. When we look closer, what we really see embedded in this perspective is not the makings of a natural transformation, but a battle where we are at war with only ourselves.

We all know how it goes: We blame the mind for hassling us, and then we take all that frustration and vitriol and turn it around on our core selves, believing ourselves to be this very struggle while we strain to put out imaginary fires within. We shame and we cower. We resist and we fight. And man, does it feel awful when we have this sort of fragmentation going on within ourselves.

It is a battle within that just keeps knocking us down. Because of how problem-based and painful that struggle is, it's common to hear much chatter about getting rid of this ego monster and its accomplice, the mind. The thing is, though, the mind never speaking again and the ego permanently ceasing is a fantasy that only the mind could ever dream up in the first place. If our essence is divine essence, and the Divine loves and accepts all of itself, then how could the Divine seek to dominate or get rid of anything? How could oneness ever fight itself? It wouldn't—and it couldn't. It would be a hallucination. If something is simply one thing, then where is the other side or the other part to argue with?

The love that we are can surely witness parts of us die that are ready to die—like old memories, trauma, pain, beliefs, and so on—but it does not seek to destroy parts of us. Love likes to transform things, not dominate and dismiss them.

What we really mean when we talk about the "death of the ego" is that we crave a rebirth; we crave an end to the perspective we have been seeing through that doesn't nurture us and therefore doesn't take us anywhere good. We crave the death of the ego-based view, the death of attachment to the suffering, an end to being so centrally located within the head, and the rebirth of the true Self and a heart-centered life.

It's important to realize that it is an unhealthy relationship with the mind, and not the mind itself, that makes the mind feel like a prison. And likewise, it's an unhealthy relationship with the ego that makes the ego seem like a dictator. What people consider to be the problem of the ego and mind is really just an issue of perspective. Indeed, we must understand their influence in our lives and work with them in supportive ways if we are to integrate our human self and Godself into our true Self.

Meet the Ego, Your New Friend

The ego inspires the possibility of identification. It is not identity itself, but rather is like a lens that gives us the perception of having an identity because it offers us a sense of self. The function of the lens is not to make us believe we are that identity, but to simply give us a sense of self so that we may know ourselves and project our individuated perspectives into life. Within our individual perspectives are our visions, desires, and other elements that we consider to be our true Selves. I understand the ego best as a projection mechanism through which we assert our uniqueness into this world. But because we are all so hungry to know who we truly are, we began to identify with the ego because it was the first sense of self that most of us can remember. The thing is, we are not that separate self. We are each a unique perspective of the Divine—*the same oneness*—expressing itself through human form.

The simplest explanation that points best toward the truth I have come to know is that a specific entity called "ego" does not exist. It is only a name we have given to this inspiration we have to identify and project ourselves. To drive the point home, imagine realizing you have an unhealthy inspiration to make money (perhaps it is rooted in fear). Would you fight that inspiration to make money and want it to die? Of course not. You would just work on being inspired to make money from a more healthy, more pure place. Same with the ego. There is no "ego"; there is only an inspiration for identity (in its less idealized version), and an inspiration for a sense of true Self and a projection of that which we desire to create (in its divinely aligned version). In our discussion, we will work with the word *ego* and consider the way it is most commonly regarded, so that we may dismantle our understanding of it from there.

The ego is most commonly understood as the identified "I" we talked about earlier. It's the part of you that attracts the building of your self-image, including the house of adjectives and nouns that compose your identity: *I am an educated, sophisticated, sexy* woman. *I enunciate my words and showcase my intelligence wherever I go. I have killer taste in music and make sure that's the first thing people know about me. And I'm repulsed by men in jean shorts.* It's the part of you that believes you *are* that identity. It's the part of you that needs to know who you are for life to make any sense. Out of balance, you are dependent upon that identity, letting its preservation guide your life, take it very seriously, and even decorate it. It's the part that says, "Who am I if I am not X or Y?" When that is happening, you will find yourself believing the way you see things is the way they really are.

The ego inspires the illusion of separateness and rightness. Without this illusion of separation, there would be no need to stand out or to have an individual identity. And without this illusion of rightness, that identity would be invalid. It's also the part of you that's inspired to prove yourself or your point again and again—the part of you that needs to be validated.

When you consider that your core essence is divine essence, and that divine essence is all that *oneness* God bliss, and ego is based in a *separate* identity that can only exist in *duality*, then you can see how there could be a conflict. For example, if you believe yourself to be who you think you are, your ego will kick up, and resistance will follow whenever oneness comes near. Why? Because the oneness obliterates the twoness the identity depends on, making unconditional love and divinity the ultimate threat.

When your sense of self is rooted in identity, there's an inherent fear and stop mechanism toward anything that makes you disappear into the stars. The identified ego would rather know itself as the banker or the yogi or the "successful one" or the always-nurturing parent because to dissolve would be to lose that specialness and that little bit that you believe you understand about yourself. So it twists and squeals and writhes and moans when oneness is near because it perceives that oneness as death, even though the death that follows oneness is the rebirth of our dreams. It's a fool's gold situation where materialism and identity are the faux and mystery and the unknown are the real.

The ego also serves to keep us alive, which to us humans means being safe and loved. Sounds great, right? Well, let's look at how this can actually play out. To begin, let's consider that neuroscience has estimated that approximately 95 percent of the mind is subconscious, which means we have no conscious idea what's going on in there—and would be shocked if we did. Briefly, the subconscious mind is where the original imprints of programming, including our habits, beliefs, patterns, and so on, are stored. Biologist and author Bruce Lipton has said that we operate 95 to 99 percent of our lives from subconscious programs.

The ego and mind, which includes both our conscious and subconscious mind, work together through a system of resonance. What this means is that if you associate that unconditional spiritual love with danger (which, as discussed, is a basic belief of an identified ego), then the ego and/or mind will try to keep you away from true intimacy in all its forms because it perceives the vibration of love as a threat to your existence. Or if you identify yourself with being a perfect mother, lover, or friend, then your ego and/or mind will inspire you to be unreceptive to actually seeing where you could "do better." Instead, it will attract conscious and subconscious thoughts that only validate your identity and its beliefs so that you may continue to believe you are that perfect mother, lover, friend. Those self-preserving thoughts are often directed toward whomever shares information that potentially invalidates your beliefs or whomever offers you a reflection of where they feel you could grow—like, "Well, you never listen. Why would I trust what you're saying?" or "She's a terrible mother. I'm not interested in her insight." So the ego attracts thought forms into the subconscious mind to prevent its own death, which is the death of the perspective of identification and which—when we believe ourselves to be the identified "I"—we subconsciously fear as our very own, finalistic death.

The inspiration to identify is not without its gifts. You may not like the outcomes of this ego inspiration, but it is not malicious. It is very benevolent—it is attempting to *protect* you so that you may continue to exist as that which you believe yourself to be. Which is what you want, right? Nope! Not once you wake up and remember who you truly are! This is why one of the most powerful things you can do is illuminate yourself about how you work.

Your relationship with the ego, or your inspiration to identify, is out of balance when you have an identity and believe it to be the truth of who you are. It's also out of balance when that identity and the inspiration to continue identifying are the lenses through which you interact with life. When you are based in the ego, your attention and energy are predominantly located within it, and all scales tip in favor of protecting your identity again and again. With that understanding, we can see how instead of breaking or getting rid of the ego, it would be more helpful to simply support the inspiration to identify to become redirected to oneness and love, which is the truth of who we are and our true "identity." If you want to know who you truly are, you have got to give up the fake stuff.

How does the reroute from ego to heart happen? As you notice yourself speaking, reacting, or existing in an ego-based state, you can make the choice to slow down and redirect your energy. I like to describe this process as bringing our energy down from our head and home to our heart. It is a retraining of our energy that requires us to check in with ourselves, notice where our attention is, and let our energy drop from the head and back into our hearts, our bodies, and the present moment.

This retraining is rooted in nonreactivity and slowing down. The more we catch ourselves and choose to consciously redirect our focus back to the present moment, simply existing as the witness of our lives, sensing and responding from the heart, fully feeding and allowing that which comes, the more we break the condition. Eventually, our inner system can become restructured, and our energy anchors and holds in our hearts and bodies more naturally and easily. This restructuring may happen in an instant or over the course of years, because transformation takes place entirely out of the time-space continuum.

You always unconditionally have the opportunity to clarify and redirect any egoic inspiration you may have to identify from the head to the heart. Remember, a healthy sense of self keeps you focused on what you are projecting into this world and inspired to know your true Self. Indeed, you can totally be inspired by your sense of self or "have an ego" without being identified with it. The simple "I" presence within that recognizes your interconnectedness with all things, and, at the same time, your individual nature and perspective as a unique channel of that oneness we all share is your only true "identity." While the ego inspires the formation of identity, it is not completely dependent upon your identification with it. Your sense of self survives as a core aspect of your humanness, the sense of individuated self. Welcome it.

Meet the Mind, Your Other New Friend

The mind is an abstract, infinite network of mathematics and sound—a vast, creative matrix of opportunity, a bountiful treasure chest of possibilities. There is only one great mind, and no one has his or her own mind. What people think of as their own mind is simply the repertoire of thoughts they have or anything that enters their space as a thought form. These thoughts do not belong to us, they are not indigenously ours; we are simply picking up on possibilities within the great spectrum of thought.

Interestingly (and certainly to the dismay of countless psychiatrists), there is no such thing as an unhealthy mind. Rather, there can only be an unhealthy relationship with the mind. There is an unhealthy relationship with the mind when you believe what it says and your reality is both based within it and guided by its dictation.

When your reality is based in your head, you perceive a distorted experience of life. In this scenario, you are giving your power away to molding thought patterns, conditions, beliefs, fear, and so on. When you live like this, you live out and experience a limited potential of intimacy and knowingness of all things, including life, your true Self, and love.

The mind may *seem* inherently unhealthy because of its tendency to offer seemingly random, unrelated, and crazy thoughts—and at all different paces and all manners of style—but this is actually very normal. Consider the mind like an antenna picking up a variety of information. The thoughts you have do not arise from your own special individuated mind—they are not yours. Sometimes, the thoughts that pass through the mind are just psychic dust we pick up from the atmosphere we are in. Other times, they are creative, incessant streams of association; responses to triggers; vibrational matches to our beings or our surroundings; or a miscellaneous mystery.

What we can really work magic with, and understand ourselves infinitely better through, is this: the mind responds to our consummate beings, which includes our feelings, our ego, our physical state, our prayers, our visions, and our intentions. The mind fills that which we are focused upon with thoughts that support the existence and progress of that focus or—*gasp!*—with thoughts that support our survival *against* the possibility of that which is being focused upon, as beliefs and memories from the subconscious are triggered and the ego kicks in to ensure survival. For example, if you associate money with evilness, then your ego will raise beliefs from the mind (I repeat: whether conscious or subconscious) that will prevent you from attracting an abundance of money. As another example, too many of us gorgeous souls are threatened by intimacy. If your system has identified intimacy as a threat, then your mind is going to enforce particular conditions and programs and spew a litany of beliefs, ideas, memories, and thoughts to keep you the hell away from it. Then, in turn, those beliefs, ideas, and so on vibrate within the body, because the mind and body are connected and everything has a vibration. The experience of your mind indeed reflects and manifests through your body, too (and vice versa).

The mind is agonized over as an uncontrollable geyser or abyss of thoughts that keep you distracted, anxious, nervous, in fear, in the past, in the future, and anywhere but here, now. Essentially, it is blamed for getting between you and the potential of your life. And when the mind is going and going and going, and you are on the train rolling and rolling, careening downhill and teetering off the tracks, what happens? It begins to skid, electrifying the tracks in an uncontrollable way, and at that point, it feels very difficult to jump off to safety.

The deeper we are in the mind, the harder it can seem to get out of it. The chatter it provides, on a sentient level, feels like the very opposite of the fabric of our being, which is silence. This is why we need to be very careful with that which we give energy and attention to at the earliest stages of getting aboard a train of thought.

Often, when something comes up, there is a critical moment where we are watching ourselves, and we are aware we have a choice: to either get onboard with the limiting thoughts and ideas of the mind or to hold ourselves in presence. The sooner we anchor deep in presence and come back to the simplicity of the now, the better. Once we get on the train of thoughts and reactivity, we enter into that unhealthy relationship with the mind, where the mind is having a conversation with itself, and it can convincingly seem quite challenging to just relax into the present moment. Therefore, in that critical moment, upon being triggered or indulging in thought and story, when we are still seeing the choices we have, it is crucial that we choose presence and the movement toward the simplicity of it all, which is always revealed in our deep inner stillness. We owe it to ourselves and to our clarity to root deep in the moment and not give in to the temptations of the mind. And, just as much, we owe it to ourselves to be compassionate with ourselves when we notice that, oops, our sleeve caught onto the caboose, and we're being dragged along the tracks once again.

If an unhealthy relationship with the mind is when we give away our power to the beliefs and thoughts that surface again and again, then a healthy relationship with the mind is one where we hold our power by remaining present and witness the mind's activity with selective interaction. In this way, the mind has the chance to reveal the limiting thoughts that are still attracting us, and with that knowledge we can make great and liberating changes within. For example, if I notice I am constantly attracted to the thought "I never get it right," then I become more aware that I am still learning how to trust myself. And with that awareness comes the choice and, then, the decision to pull my energy away from that thought and into the sense of trust within, and perhaps to also explore whatever modality of healing I feel may support me in my resolution and alignment.

A healthy relationship with the mind also assists us in creating and sharing the expression of our clarity, our truth, and our heart. This sort of good relationship with the mind is the most magical gift. In this good-relationship context, the mind is like a divine servant that provides us with the solutions, steps, aha! moments, and ideas to create that which we are aligned to create and desire to create, which we announce to existence by virtue of our attentiveness and where we are focused. Existence interprets our prayerful attention as a command to manifest. Because we are the Divine and the Divine is us, as we announce our visions to ourselves with conviction, so, too, are they supported by all of existence.

Through the possibility of healthy thoughts, such as, "Of course I can do this" and "I am completely supported in doing this," we conspire with the mind through the technique of dialoguing with the universe and the world around us on an energetic level. Through the mind, we can visualize that which we are inspired to create. Through our visualization, we announce what we are focusing upon and establish the vibration of that which we are drawing toward ourselves. The mind is part of the total picture of creation, and it is an irreplaceable tool in this human experience. When we partner with it in awareness, the mind is a wonderful co-conspirator in manifesting the life of our divine visions.

What a game changer, isn't it? If the thoughts that pass through the mind aren't inherently ours and they exist in all possibilities, why not choose those that support us and either dismiss the rest or work with them for our wholeness? If we have the opportunity to work with the totality of our being—mind included—in our embodiment of peace and freedom and our creative potential in this life, why not run to the front of *that* line?

Let me be clear: I am not suggesting that we change our thoughts and beliefs like some sort of oversimplified panacea magic trick. Rather, I'm pointing out the importance of understanding how it all works. If there are old emotional patterns, trauma, wounds, and so on, then simply resolving beliefs related to that old pain is not always enough. We must deal with things at their root.

Let's explore other ways to reawaken to the understanding of nonreactivity and rooting into our presence enough that we can conspire with the mind, rather than being dominated by it.

Your Attention Is Your Power

As lively as your thoughts may seem, they are ineffective and inert without your attention. Understand that your attention is a life giver for all things in your life, including the thoughts that pass through your mind. The ones you focus upon, believe, and interact with—those are the ones that become real. The ones you simply witness without interaction become starved and eventually either disappear or become inaudible, inconsequential—and recognized as nothing more than impersonal phenomena.

You are the God essence of all things in your life, and you get to choose which thoughts manifest in your reality. Energize the good ones with your agreement and belief, but not the ones that do not serve you. Energize the ones that are a supportive, creative dialogue with life, but not the ones that boost you artificially.

Energize thoughts of doubt and fear, and you will experience the subsequent chapters of that story. Let those moments pass while reorienting your attention away from the thoughts and into the present moment, and you will be choosing love. You will be choosing truth. The thoughts will simply leave without causing any damage. And the sun will rise again, as it always does, and you will live to see the flowers opening another day.

Trusting that all of this benevolent creation goes on even when the clouds are dark and looming, even when challenging thoughts and triggers come—holding yourself in that majestic seat of presence, slowing down, orienting again and again toward inner silence—is what makes all the difference. This is the game changer. Your deepest nature knows just what weather is needed for your garden to grow and evolve, and you will get that. If you give in to fear and unnecessary doubt, the flowers may wilt. And if they wilt, that will be fine, because who wants their life to blossom upon a foundation still filled with poison? Ah, the gardening work of life! The ceremony of it all! This is our mastery.

Choosing Your Narrative: It's Not Your Thoughts, It's What You Do with Them

As a consequence of their influence, the mind and the ego have been blamed for all sorts of life and relationship issues. Consider: You're in an argument with your partner (or your mother, father, child), and you find yourself trying to prove your point or explain yourself over and over again to demonstrate just how right you are. Or perhaps you are so intent on the discussion because you want to be understood. Later, when you cool off, what do you realize? Perhaps, "Argh, I did it again. My dreadful ego—always making me justify myself and explain myself and causing all sorts of problems!" That's a fairly common response from one who is trying to get a better grip on the reins. Or perhaps that's not what you realize. Perhaps you are still moving into clarity about how the mind and ego can influence you.

Either way, let's glean a bit more clarity about the real issue. It is not your ego, and it is not your mind. Remember, they only have as much power as you give them. It's how we—*as awareness itself*—deal with them. It's the narrative we choose to construct from the thoughts that surface. So what you are witnessing is not the cruel power of the mind and the ego at play. No, what you are witnessing is simply your *reactivity* to them and the fact that you've given them any power at all.

When you're stuck in this game of blaming the ego and mind, you are in a box that needs to burn. Your mind and your ego are not the problem. Keep believing they are, and you will continue to miss the real issue. Wherever there is blame, there is illusion. Wherever there is desperation to be understood, there is the illusion of being separate from the Divine.

When we start to realize the gifts of a healthy relationship with the ego and the mind, we realize that part of the ceremony, part of the spiritual practice of life, is actually about how we interact with them, how we work with the reflections of ourselves that we see through their projection, and how we live with them together as one.

Let's say you have lived with two friends, Amy and Samantha, for one year, and that during that year, you've cooked 80 percent of all dinners. Your roommates both contribute to paying for the food, so no issue there; but nearly every time you are all together for dinner, Samantha prepares the ingredients, you cook, and Amy cleans up.

Normally, you don't think much about it, but on this particular night, you watch Samantha start with the garlic on the chopping board, and you become enraged inside. Thoughts come: "What the fuck? Does she not know how to put the stove on? Is there something so hard about sautéing vegetables? Would it be impossible for her to find the inspiration to actually cook a meal? And Amy—oh, Amy—always getting the good end of the stick—loving the dinner she's served and just cleaning up, whistling as she goes. Thanks so much, Amy—that's *really* helpful. *Argh!*"

Here is that critical moment we talked about earlier—the moment you see yourself starting to brim. Are you going to believe the thoughts that have come? Are you going to pick up some plates and start smashing them against the wall? Are you going to believe this victim narrative and tell off your friends? Are you, in any way, going to buy into the blame and energetic charge of these thoughts? Or are you going to take a few deep breaths and realize something deeper must be happening? Something deeper that's being reflected back to you through the holy mirror of perception.

Perhaps on this particular night you've become annoyed with the dynamic because you wish someone were taking care of you for a change. After all, you have been feeling a bit down about the abrupt end to a new connection with a guy you'd been dating. And only a few hours ago you had a long conversation with your mother, whom you rarely speak to, and she was putting you down for "another failed relationship" and treating you just like she always has, blaming you for the things that "go wrong" in your life, leaving you alone to make all of your own meals since you were twelve while she went out on dates.

Oh, wait a second . . .

So are you going to rage out with the thoughts? Are you going to act out and react to them? Or are you going to take care of yourself by staying present and accepting the anticlimactic realization that everything in front of you is actually fine? "Hey, cooking is therapy for me at the end of the day. And besides, I really don't enjoy the meals the two of them make. Samantha is happy to chop the vegetables, which I can't stand to do. And Amy loves to clean, which I'd also rather not do. We actually have a pretty good dynamic and flow. I can let them know how grateful I'd be if they'd order in for us, and excuse myself from making dinner tonight, if that's what I need." This is the narrative you can choose to develop on this particular night—the narrative that has you looking at what is happening in the present moment at face value and then either taking a time-out immediately or later on, in a good moment for you, to self-reflect and tend to the unresolved feelings that rest beneath the trigger. It is a narrative that transcends narrative and becomes open, loving space once again.

Often, when we are triggered, what we are witnessing is simply our subconscious attraction to a story, and that attraction is there because we believe that story still serves us. It's attempting to teach us something that we desire to learn and helping us to purge unresolved feelings. Through the reflection of seeing how our mind projects a whole ordeal on a benign moment, we see what is going on within *ourselves* and not what is going on in *reality*.

As a disclaimer, I must add that we can certainly become angry, sad, and so on as a response (and not a reaction) to a present situation—not all emotions are related to the past or the result of a distortion. For example, if you were walking your dog and someone started kicking him, it would be a natural response to become angry. However, what we're focusing on here are emotional triggers related to that which is unresolved within.

When we know what the mind is about, we know it's not going to feel love or understand the mysteries of life or tell us why things are the way they are, or even bring us a sense of lasting satisfaction, because we know that's not what it does. Likewise, when we realize the ego identity has got some serious tricks up its sleeves, we can be hip to that and remain alert to keep our energy balanced. And with all of this understanding about how our inner world works, we can choose to create a great narrative for our lives by bringing the mind and ego into partnership with our consummate Selves. We can work with the gifts of each part to create the epic visions of our lives.

Indeed, we can move into unity consciousness with our ego intact and our feet on the ground, so why not work with it for our freedom and for the making of great magic in our lives? Why not work with all of the ingredients of ourselves and our lives to choose and create the ultimate vision of our human life, as presented, suggested, and offered to us by the Divine? Taking our consummate Selves and our lives here for granted is not an act of the heart or an embodiment of truth. Since when is Earth inferior to the Divine? Since when is the spiritual experience of the human not good enough as it is? To say the least, life here is incredibly, gloriously, unfathomably sacred and precious. It is here, on Earth, as humans, that we meet the Guru of Life.

Whatever You Choose Is Okay with God

The ego is a brilliant generator that introduces us to a sense of self, and the mind is an absolute treasure chest. We may not always like what their influence inspires, but they are not malicious. This is why we must understand and embrace how we work, because if we do not intelligently work *with* our system, things will likely continue to play out in a way we don't truly, consciously desire and intend. Remember, in the eyes of God, *it's all good*. To God, to the Divine, simply because something is happening, it is fine as it is. To God, to exist, to happen, to be or not be is enough! No reasons, no purposes necessary. God is pure love, and pure love does not have an agenda. It simply overflows and creates. It simply is.

Divine essence is not judgmental. It does not view one experience as better than another. However you choose to learn and whatever you choose to experience as a result of how you engage with yourself and with life is totally fine to the Divine, simply because it is happening, period. Everything and anything that happens or does not happen is always in a process of synchronization and harmonization with everything else. So if you want to believe you are your thoughts, that is fine to the Divine. And to humanize this all a bit, I remind you that even then, even when your mind won't shut up or something feels awful or wrong or completely uncomfortable, there is always something to learn, appreciate, and grow from, even if the invitation is simply to let yourself be.

Whatever marching orders the *all* of you—mind, body, and spirit—gives, you'll get the results. If they're conflicting, you'll get conflicting results, like attracting that good relationship but then running away and calling it quits when things get too real. The key is to move into the space of intelligence of your entire system—into knowing how your mechanism works—so you can begin to work with it instead of against it and untangle what needs to be untangled. How can it be said any other way? *You* are the divine intervention you have been waiting for.

Understanding Resonance, Your Mechanism, and Your Choices

Do you know the song "November Rain" by Guns N' Roses? Or "Mad World" by Gary Jules? Both are very maudlin, emotional, sad songs. If you don't know these songs, just consider another song that is very sad.

Now, even if you got rid of the lyrics, those songs still evoke a feeling of emotional sensitivity and sadness, right? Why is that? It's because certain musical notes and sequences of musical notes actually trigger certain feelings. Why? *Because of their resonance.* Every feeling has a certain vibration, which corresponds to a sound. It is math. It is one of the blueprints of existence.

The mind (and the rest of you), naturally, is subject to this math and works the same way. Something happens: your partner pisses you off, your boss yells at you, your mother does that thing she always does. You are triggered. The trigger stimulates an emotion: maybe it is anger, hopelessness, sadness, frustration, feelings of unworthiness. A feeling has arrived, a resonance has risen, and you are vibrating in tune with that. By virtue of being connected to all things and the great one mind, you begin to pick up thoughts that resonate with your vibration. If they are feelings of unworthiness or hopelessness, then perhaps the thoughts are something like, "I'm always alone. It's never going to work out." You are picking up thoughts and other feelings like this because you are one beautiful mathematical creature, and you are subject to the laws of existence.

And on and on it goes, and none of it is personal. These thoughts may seem very personal—as if they are truly yours and about you—but in fact they aren't. These thoughts surface simply because of the laws of existence, never because they are describing the indelible truth of you. The only thing that is personal (if ever there were something) is *what you are choosing*. Are you choosing to react or buy into the thoughts, or are you choosing to hold yourself in presence? Are you choosing to beat yourself up when you catch yourself reacting, or are you choosing to reorient into the compassion of the present moment? To me, this is the ultimate question: *What are you choosing?*

So, you are picking up on thoughts because of your momentary vibration, and whatever you choose projects the direction of your vibration, which just means the next moment that comes is created by your present moment and what are you focusing upon. It is more simple than it sounds: If you react, then you are going into reactivity. If you hold yourself in presence, then you are going forward in deeper presence. If you choose to believe the thought that "this is hopeless," then subsequent thoughts will arise to support that belief, like "No matter what I do, we always end up fighting."

Whatever thought you choose to believe invites the next thought, and if you've got a room packed with drunken co-eds on a Friday night, do you think a middle-aged lady walking home from a book club meeting will be invited in? Thoughts that are believed are homogenous and are attracted to each other like that. If you choose one and then two and then three, then they are going to attract more of their own kind into the room until it's so packed you have to squeeze through just to get to the bathroom. Until they become their own sort of herd mentality. If thoughts you attach to create a crowded room, then you can consider the unattached mind space like a room with open windows and a constant breeze, where anything you do not engage with or explicitly invite to stay for an inquisition over tea eventually passes out the windows without a problem.

We must remember that life is synchronistic. Energy is always harmonizing, even when it is moving apart or seems discordant. What that means is that when we are dwelling in a marsh of limiting thoughts, it will always get thicker and thicker until our presence takes over, because more limiting thoughts and corresponding life coincidences will be synchronistic and resonant and attracted. And on and on it goes until we, ourselves, step in, once again, as the divine intervention.

The Simple Way

All there is to do is witness that which passes, just like you notice clouds as they move and shift, and as they thunder, storm, and disappear. You are the sky that witnesses, and the thoughts are clouds—simply phenomena. When unsupportive thoughts come out of habit, repertoire, and resonance, what is there to do but witness them and remain still, silent, and focused upon the truth within, upon the breath? By holding your presence, breathing toward the inner direction of silence, and not energizing the thoughts, you will be offering and introducing a new way of being to your inner system. When you modify the way you interact with your mind, your life will change in miraculous ways. And then, life can be like a magical kaleidoscope you are having the pleasure of being poetically transformed by.

When inspiring thoughts come, like when you are listening to a great song or looking at the waves of the ocean, and you think, "Wow, this life is beautiful!" or "Ah, I feel like calling Catrine and telling her how much I love her," why not go for it? Why not let those thoughts stoke the fire of your heart? If your inner voice, your intuition, is responding with, "Yeah, this is the moment for that," then it's your responsibility to yourself to follow that. In the ceremony of life, anything that deepens your truth, your alignment, your flow, and your expression is welcome and needed—and honoring it is honoring the ceremony of life.

When our hearts, our truths, are directing our energy, we are where we need to be. Then we move out of the embodiment of our minds and into the embodiment of our Selves. Then our mind is a divine tool, an epic computer utilized to create that which we truly desire and intend to create. I can't say it enough: a sharp, healthy mind is invaluable. The key is for the heart to be in charge. It has been said many times before that when the mind, is the master, there are problems. When the heart is the master and the mind its servant, we are in good shape. Literally, good shape comes into our lives.

Maybe you dream of a life where there is less accountability for your choices. But this dream is just that: a dream. You contain within you all the energy of God, and so you will see how powerful you are, whether you like what you are giving life to or not. Things will never be rearranged for you just because you *want* them to be. To move into this deeper empowerment requires an intimacy with life, a deep engagement and maturity. It requires you stepping into the fact that *you, yourself,* are the divine force you've been both praying for and praying to.

And so what we see is that rather than being an overwhelming responsibility, this power of choice is actually liberation. It is our liberation in action. To live and create like this—so intentionally, so powerfully—this is the gift of life and the true Self. This is our exalted song.

Chapter 7

FROM SELF-DENIAL
TO SELF-ACCEPTANCE

Keep walking, though there's no place to get to.
Don't try to see through the distances.
That's not for human beings. Move within,
but don't move the way fear makes you move.

RUMI, *The Essential Rumi* (Coleman Barks, translator)

We must understand self-denial if we are to illuminate and free up the mysterious ways we have shut ourselves down. During this ceremony of perpetual blossoming, as we fine-tune our beings to be the open channels of receiving and expressing that we inherently are, it is likely we will meet many blocks within. Much of this energetic congestion is the consequence of self-denial. If we're going to move into the integrated, empowered way of being we've been talking about, then we need to talk about self-denial. We need to call it out so it can be noticed and moved from the darkness into the light.

Self-denial exists in two forms: denying primal urges and denying your true Self. The first leads to the second. Textbook self-denial begins as a repression of an urge, which, over the years, grows into an inability to express or even know your true voice.

Why do we deny primal and natural urges in the first place? Most often, because somebody—perhaps our parents, our peers, or a religious figure—told us those urges were wrong. Somebody told us that to do X would be unacceptable. And if we did something unacceptable, we quite literally would not be accepted by others in our natural way of being, which is the natural way energy moves through us and our natural way of expressing and exploring life. From there, if we were unaccepted, we were denied love, because love is all-inclusive. If the "unacceptable" urge was related to a specific part of ourselves, then we likely chose to cut ourselves off from that part. The belief that only certain parts of us are lovable and acceptable led us to become fragmented, "normal," incomplete—less than our true Selves. This is the general way many of us learned to stop trusting ourselves.

How can we trust ourselves if our natural flow, our natural way of being, leads to rejection, shame, judgment, and ridicule? It is much more pleasant and gratifying (or so it seems) to modify our natural behavior in order to be loved. It is a trade-off. To be accepted and loved, we became submissive, conditioned, and fragmented.

The thing is, that trade-off only makes sense to the rational mind and its storage house, the subconscious mind, neither of which are antennas to truth. While it may seem like suppressing certain parts of ourselves results in us being more loved, that can never happen. Love is total, 100 percent of the time. As children, we depended on the adults around us, and so we learned to associate love with survival. We were only ever trying to remain loved and safe, and now that we are becoming aware of how our inner mechanisms are working, we are in a much stronger position to untangle and move through them.

Here's an example of where self-denial can begin and how to make a turnaround. Consider the religious culture of shame around masturbation. If a prepubescent boy is given space and privacy to sexually explore himself, all other factors aside, he's more likely to naturally develop into a sexually healthy teen. He'll likely further explore his sexual urges and eventually become a healthy adult and move into a more mature connection with his sexual energy. However, if that same boy is told to repress, judge, and ignore these urges, and he actually does, he can become dysfunctional and ill—not only because it is vital that one's sexual energy is known and explored, but also because to shame our very nature has disheartening consequences. (I am simplifying here for the sake of isolating the importance of denial versus acceptance.)

Other examples of the origins of self-denial could include a child being discouraged from playing music, or a young boy being discouraged from helping his mother make clothes and told to play ball. The discouragement always has strings attached to it; otherwise, how could it exist at all? A parent's discouragement of their child is always loaded. It is always seen as an "if X, then Y" situation, such as, "If you masturbate, then God will be angry with you" or "If you sew with your mother instead of playing ball, then I will reject you (because I find your feminine qualities repulsive)." Even if parents never actually say, "If you do X, then Y will happen," that's still how children interpret and store the situation within the subconscious mind. Never forget that children are picking up the patterns and cues of their environment, including what their parents judge to be acceptable or unacceptable, safe or unsafe expressions, actions, and feelings, from the moment they are born.

The examples just mentioned have secondary connections to sexuality. Why? Because children's pleasure, enjoyment, and inspiration comes from their primal impulse and nature of being turned on, in a lit-up-by-life way, and that turn-on involves the same energy centers that include sexuality. When a kid who gets turned on by playing music is punished for it or told not to do it, and therefore represses the divine desire to do so, an energetic dysfunction often takes root. And thus begins the path of denying our true nature.

The need to scream, cry, and move our bodies in order to shift and release energy are also primal needs. When children are told to repress any of these natural tendencies, they are likely to also repress them in their adult life because there will be a painful imprint (like rejection, humiliation, or shame) around these natural, intuitive ways of transmuting energy and healing.

It is critical that we allow our energy to move however it needs. As we begin to acknowledge and address these needs, we may choose to participate in yoga, tai chi, dance, or one of the other countless ways we can honor and support the intuitive movement of energy through our bodies. When we deny the impulse to shift and release energy, the energy accumulates and becomes pent up inside of us. Other than being unhealthy, this interferes with the flow of our true expression, which relates to the denial of our true Self. So please, get in the car, go for a drive, and scream your lungs out if you need to.

From these very first moments of learning to deny ourselves, wherever these moments are stored within us, a distortion arises that alters our perspective. A self-limiting condition takes hold that keeps us from being our true Self and trusting life. How can we trust life if it made us this way and being this way makes us unaccepted and unloved? Without even knowing it, we deploy subconscious control mechanisms and programming to ensure we behave in ways that keep us accepted and loved. Doing so connects to the ego, as it attempts to protect our sense of self, and to the mind, as it repeats to us the story we resonate with and believe we need—the story from which we are learning.

The denial of primal urges can also begin through more intense experiences, such as abuse, neglect, or trauma. All abuse, neglect, and traumatic childhood experiences encourage us to *not* trust our instinct or life or God, because the subconscious connects the dots that any or all three are responsible for getting us in that awful situation to begin with. There are also secondary beliefs and associations that result from such experiences, but they are specific to each situation. For example, if a child is sexually abused, then they learn that sexual energy puts them in danger (and danger, for many who have been abused, is often a "safe" place because it's what we know—it's familiar). That distortion can manifest in many different ways, but when there has been sexual abuse, the interpretation in the subconscious will most often (if not always) include the message that one's sexual energy is unsafe. All of this unresolved trauma takes a perfectly healthy, sweet child and turns him or her into a shut-down adult (even if that wounding is only noticed in certain areas).

The good news is that, as conscious adults, we are extremely empowered by the choices we make. Our focal point now is, as always, how we work with the reflection of ourselves that we see, including any old wounds and destructive behavior. Do we ignore the limitations and continue to let them either silence us or influence us to act out? Or do we work with them in our ceremony as an invitation to purify the channels that we are? When they arise, do we push them more deeply down into our bodies and minds, or do we address them, gently, compassionately, as we would a child—*the inner child*—to find out what they *really* need, what's *really* going on?

As it relates to self-denial, whatever is being resisted or denied needs to first be understood. When the simple urge to cheat on your spouse, or to run away, or to hurt another or oneself, or even to take what isn't yours, is not judged, shamed, or demonized, there is much more space to get to the core issue and, from there, into resolution. Then we are more inclined to feel it is safe to share the feelings with someone who can help, if need be. Then the urge can be explored, and the trapped issue within the urge can move toward the light. Indeed, when we offer ourselves to the harbor of unconditional love, we are reminded of its power to transform even the most impenetrable and impossible of things.

Historically, people have been given religious and cultural prescriptions for dealing with their "digressions." However, no formula could ever honor or touch that which is truly lurking within. Only presence, attention, and love can. The typical formula for repentance and apology says, "Hey, this is ugly. Quickly say or do this and promise to control yourself, and you're forgiven. And I can look at you again. We'll pretend it never happened. We can go on with our lives." It pushes those urges and parts of ourselves deemed unacceptable further into the darkness of shame.

To move things into darkness is to judge them and repress your nature, which is the opposite of exploring and trusting your nature—your spiritual nature. To move things into this darkness is to act out of connection with God. It is to attempt to alter the natural fabric of God. If you are with God, or if you are moving toward remembering your unity with God, then trust that which the Divine creates. Be willing to see the gold within it. Explore it and move it into the light. Make everything welcome.

For addressing and moving through what's really going on within, acceptance is required. We need to be willing to accept ourselves in totality, with all our darkness and light, before we can really purify the big stuff. We are all of that—the good, the bad, and the ugly. And we are none of that: we are that which transcends, that which remains, that which witnesses the good, the bad, the ugly. When we accept all that is within us—including all possibilities of all the duality of this life—and are willing to see it for what it is, then we are really in a place to let it go and realize we were actually never *that* at all.

It is through our acceptance of ourselves, as we are, that the old energetic pathways of denial are liberated. Denial is the dam that imposes itself upon the river and diverts the natural flow of the water. What happens? The river dries up, the flora disappears, and the wildlife stops visiting where the water was once thriving and flowing. Self-acceptance is the love that obliterates that artificial dam. Through this compassion for ourselves, the water flows again and heals the parts of us that had been deserted and dried out.

The only way out is in. As denial is liberated back into love, the soft, incandescent gaze of compassion is what we see in the mirror. Through the exploration of denial in whatever form it exists within us, we will discover the deepest acceptance that rests quietly in the core of all that's been holding us back.

When we shift our orientation from denial of ourselves to acceptance of ourselves (even if it begins as an effort or a practice), we embrace that which comes up. We stay alert in the moments when imprisonment could begin, vigilant in the moments when we are triggered and the wounds and blockages may take over. This attention requires great dedication, vulnerability, and humility. By and by, we chisel away at the hold of the mind and the grip of our patterns and fears through our reorientation, our new choices, and the ground from which we move. Through our constant reorientation to the moment and our willingness to see ourselves as we truly are, the truth inevitably rises to the surface.

Let's consider a practical example of what self-acceptance can look like—a gentle example that most (if not all) of us can relate to. You're on your third date with Chris. You really like him and have been looking forward to going out with him all week. You're two hours into dinner, having an amazing time, looking into his melty brown eyes as the two of you laugh, when, all of a sudden, it hits you: You're wide open. You're vulnerable. Your heart is sensitive, and you are exposed.

An uncomfortable self-awareness has arrived, for you are not comfortable with what you see. The core need to be loved has been touched, and its rawness is translated into the need to protect and the impulse to contract. Your body starts to react, and the thought avalanche begins: "He must be noticing how into him I am, and, oh man, is this going to turn him off? Am I too available too soon? What if I end up getting hurt?" In response to your mind, the urge to contract your heart gets stronger and stronger.

Now—critical moment—what do you do? In this moment, you have caught yourself and become self-aware, so what choice do you make? It's go time. Do you allow the fear to shut you down and deny your true expression and your true Self, or do you choose to breathe more deeply into the urge to contract, allowing yourself to open your heart more, like your life depends on it? (Because, after all, it does.)

You can, in fact, continue to stay open and in this beautiful dialogue with this man whilst being in a space of pristine rawness and sensitivity. Carrying on in presence and letting yourself be seen in the beauty of your vulnerability is a strength, and this authenticity helps to resolve the core issue: the belief that you need to close down your true Self in order to be safe and loved. You can even share your fear and your urge to close down with Chris, if it feels right. If he's worth his salt, he'll love you for it.

In these moments, when the impulse to contract is triggered and the memories, beliefs, and thoughts that trigger self-denial arrive, the ultimate invitation that we receive again and again throughout the ceremony has come: stay present and breathe. You have the option to accept the presence of it all, including the parts of yourself you're afraid of showing and the impulse to contract and hide, even if it takes some trying and getting used to. It can feel extremely hard to open in the face of the fear, so be gentle with yourself in your journey to opening. After all, your evolution and your expansion include your contraction. Opening and expanding do not always need to happen, and it's important to remember and honor that. Sometimes the most profound openings happen after strong contractions (like childbirth).

Indeed, to know the true Self, we have got to be real, and the truth is that we're not radiance and sunshine all the time. We're not open-heart magic love beams taking the world by storm all day, every day. Rather, we are more like flowers, and without a doubt, every garden is equally nourished by the solemnness of night and the vitality of day. Every garden prospers by virtue of being rooted in the messy, powerful earth and energized by the life-giving sun. Just stay present with what's happening, listen to and honor what you need as best you can, and you will be in the miracle of your authenticity and your mastery.

This is the way of practicing acceptance of yourself and moving forward through the tunnels of self-denial and into your sweet and gentle heart. You do the same when the temptation to hide and shut down comes in any other moment of self-expression and openness, like singing in front of others, dancing, sharing your poetry at an open mic, or expressing your boundaries or your pain. You carry on despite it all, and by virtue of the incredible strength of love it takes to persevere, everything takes care of itself. This is the power of love—this is you being your own divine intervention. By moving forward anyway, the issue naturally begins to resolve, and you eventually see that expressing yourself as you are meant to only *enhances* your ability to love and be loved.

We must move the way love makes us move. Rather than resenting the urges and the pain, we begin to treat ourselves like we would a sweet little child, nurturing ourselves when life gets hard. We move toward realizing how innocent the nature of our being is and that all we are really trying to do is protect ourselves and feel loved, sometimes in twisted ways. And how can we demonize that?

Self-acceptance requires feeling the hardest parts of yourself that you'd much prefer to wish away and ignore. To ignore them, though, would be to live one-tenth of a life. Often, we need support as we begin to work through the deep roots of denial. If you feel you need support from a practitioner or friend during this journey, please reach out. There are so many brilliant people and healing modalities out there that can be very helpful in times of deep transformation.

Our triggers, at their core, are completely innocent. They are not there for the purpose of controlling us or as a challenge God gave us to make us stronger. They are just showing us where something needs to move (at a vibration akin to an alarm) in order for us to be at ease and in alignment, having learned that which we are calling in to learn. Just as the body sends us signals like rashes, fever, and pain to alert us when something is physically ailing, the spiritual body is alerted through our triggers. Triggers and urges can get a bit intense in order to bring to our attention that something within us needs the salve of our awareness.

As we've discussed, many of our urges have to do with sexuality and our desire—lo, our *need*—to be turned on. We are inherently sexual beings, and until a certain moment in our evolution, we are constantly trying to be turned on. Initially, we believe this impulse and possibility comes exclusively from sexual encounters. But as we awaken from that dream, we realize that *all of life* is a turn-on and what we have been seeking was actually this totally lit-up state of being, this heart-body-soul radiance.

As we reorient our lives toward the sacred nature of all, we begin to realize that sex is offered to us as a mystical, powerful, enlightened experience rather than one that is limited to physicality or tied up in yearning, attachments, destructive subconscious attraction, and wants. We realize that sex is actually making love, and that to be with someone in this way is to share our energy in the most sensitive and powerful of ways—and that the act holds within it the potential for a profound cosmic, creative experience. After all, sexual energy is divine energy, which is meant to course through our bodies and offer us a totally expansive, transformative experience of cosmic divine vibration. Sexual energy and the energy of being turned on are both really just very electric love.

So if you, for example, cheated on your partner, what you don't need is to believe that you have sinned, dwell in a pool of misery and disdain, or cover it up. What you don't need to do is go to a religious figure who tells you that you have to repent for it or friends and family who offer only judgment, disgust, and punishment. You already know well enough how much it burns to act on destructive impulses (if you don't, chances are you would not be reading this book). Wasting time and energy in punishment is both distracting and useless. What's going to support and nourish you is sorting out why you felt the need to sleep with that person. What is out of alignment within your relationship, yourself, or your life that inspired you to make the decision to cheat rather than discuss your feelings with your partner? Why did you make a choice that hurt you? What inner needs of yours are you not tending to? (To be clear, I'm not suggesting that monogamy is the right thing for everyone; rather, I'm pointing out that circumventing issues is destructive and indicative of something deeper going on.)

No matter what has happened, no matter how much you may feel like you need forgiveness from someone else, the only person you truly need it from is yourself. God is within you, and all resolution happens inside. You are not a bad person; you have just found another one of those little flags that says, "Dig here—something unresolved needs your attention!"

The last suggestion anyone needs with regard to their triggers and unresolved issues is the threat of judgment and the instruction of repression or punishment. In fact, the very last thing you and the world at large needs is more repression and judgment. This is a very old story, a medieval story. We are in a new age, and this is the moment in time and evolution where we play catch-up with ourselves, our true Selves, and our divine nature. The reign of darkness is done; we are just catching up to the fact that it has been phased out. It's like a song that has been playing on repeat for thousands of years. Eventually it stops; eventually the machine it has been running on will just cease to function, because it will be so outdated it can no longer be held up by technology. But even after that moment we still have that song repeating in our minds. This is exactly what is happening now with our consciousness. The dynasty of darkness is over, and we are just shaking off the repetitive imprint/memory of it as we realize we are standing here, right now, draped and radiating in all the splendor and light of a million dazzling universes.

You see, life is an inherently benevolent process. When you start to view your life with even a smidgen of detachment, the curtains begin to draw back. You see that, for starters, you actually can indeed draw back the curtains, and then you see the old dusty stage set that is ready to go.

And you choose just that: You choose for it to go; you choose to purify. You choose to unshackle the gorgeous beast within, to let it out and talk to it, to see what it wants. You choose to run your fingers through its crazy, ratty hair, pulling out whatever little bugs got too cozy in there over the years. You give it a glass of water and a shower, and you show it the sun. You welcome it. All of this to say: Get to know the master within you. Fall at the feet of your Self.

BURNING THE ROPES
OF CONTROL

You often say, "I would give, but only to the deserving."
The trees in your orchard say not so, nor the flocks in your pasture.
They give that they may live, for to withhold is to perish.

KAHLIL GIBRAN, *The Prophet*

Often, we must manage our human selves if we are to honor our true Selves. Knowing that our human selves are influenced by a whole cosmos of things, we can appreciate that we must drop more and more into the Godspace within if we are to live as we truly intend. The changes we make as we shift from *what we have been doing* to *what we truly intend to be doing* could be described as "self-management," though it really means nothing more than *Self-honoring*. It's that aspect of slowing down and checking ourselves as we shift out of the perspective of the isolated self and return to the embodiment of the integrated Self.

It is important to distinguish between self-management and self-control because, to the untrained eye, they can look quite similar in their superficial appearance. For example, one can choose to be a vegetarian as a way of Self-honoring or as a way of self-control. When the decision to not eat meat arises from the intuitive voice of your being, then honoring that practice is honoring divine guidance and what's right for you. However, if you decide to become a vegetarian solely because you *think* (mental) it's the *right* thing to do (judgment), or because someone told you to (giving away your power), then that action is a form of control that inhibits your unique, divine flow. As another example, chanting mantras can be devotion for one person and distraction for another. The subject here is not those aspects of our lives that may be disciplinary in nature and therefore *look* like rules. Rather, what we're talking about is control—the imposed rules and manipulations we engage with that arise outside of our inner truth and internal resonance.

Control

Control, as it is used here, is a general term for anything we do or accept that alters how anything is naturally occurring, including our natural selves, our natural flow, others, and life. It includes the little things we do, like holding back from calling a love interest so that we may play it cool or trying to duplicate a meditation that once brought us to bliss, and the big things, like forcing ourselves to stay at a job that doesn't inspire us or staying in a relationship that's no longer right for us. We often think exercising control is a way of empowering ourselves in our lives, but in fact it's the very opposite. It sucks us dry and disempowers us, and it blocks and inhibits our intuition. Indeed, it turns us rote and robotic rather than moved by the fluid love flow of life.

We try to control things (especially ourselves) because we are afraid of what will happen if we don't, and we're afraid of ruining our lives. As previously discussed, we do it so that we may feel safe and increase the chances of being accepted and loved. To be sure, most of us were born into environments filled with people under the spell of the isolated self, and so they projected that perspective onto us. They tried to tell us how to live and what to believe and wanted us to agree with their versions of right and wrong. Without a doubt, most of us were groomed to become controlling adults and distrustful of our nature.

In addition, many of our world's religions either directly or indirectly tell us not to trust ourselves, our preferences, and our instincts, but instead to trust the direction provided by the designated person between us and God. To that end, rules have been interjected throughout religious sermons and texts, offered (or imposed) as a way to help connect us to God and to show us how to be devoted. But only someone who does not understand God could ever believe that people do not have this wisdom inside, that they need a set of rules to get it right, and that there could ever even be someone—*anything!*—between a person and supreme divinity. A true guide will always lead us back to ourselves.

Consider it: Do you really need to be told to not kill a man? And if you actually need to be told, does simply following this forbiddance as a *rule* truly help you? Of course not. Does believing you will be judged and punished if you do or do not do certain things lead you to an understanding of life, yourself, or God? No. Does following a rule of loving your neighbor keep you in the good graces of God? This is just silly. It is not possible to love your neighbor without even knowing what love is. Love yourself first. Until the love within is discovered, it is impossible to share it with another. Rules like this imply that you are separate from God and must be given a set of laws to follow in order to build and maintain your connection and good standing.

Living in harmony with God (aka your Godself) needs no mechanisms of control and no sets of rules; quite the opposite, in fact, because control contradicts your natural flow. Flow cannot happen where there are tourniquets, just as masking an issue with controlling behavior will never make it go away.

Control is, by nature, disfiguring, which is why we feel so deformed when we are in such states: because we edged out the beauty and the vitality of our truth. For example, when we force a smile in moments that we're simply not naturally inspired to smile, something feels dull. This endless micromanagement is part of the exhausting formula humans have created to convince themselves that the stability of both their identity and their life are as guaranteed and locked in as they can be, and that they are doing everything they can to be worthy of love.

When we're in control mode it's nearly impossible to catch the magic of life because we are too afraid to see it. After all, following the magic is like hopping atop a traveling rainbow, which is a very freaky thing to us when we're afraid of life. When we're still holding on to the grips we hold ourselves back from the natural ride of life at all costs for fear of what might happen to us if we let go, for fear of losing our minds and our identities. But when we allow ourselves to just exist as we are—no control, no bullshit—our beauty has space to come through and shine, and we become the graceful warriors of life that we all inherently are.

Life is wild and unpredictable, and only by appreciating that will we meet that which is unchanging within us—that which *cannot* change. Humans create all these complicated ways to feel safe and loved, but really we are looking for one thing: that which is indestructible within us, that which we can always count on—our true locus of control. A love that does not go away. The love within—unconditional love. God. Oneness. Peace. That is all we really desire—the desire within all the other *wants*. So the invitation for all the control—*to know thy Self and trust thy Self*—in the end gets demolished by the love discovered within.

Judgment

Judgment is a mechanism of control we're all familiar with, and it acts like a herd of little minions narrowing and limiting our knowingness of our worlds. Judging is interpreting our observations and creating conclusions and definitions based on that interpretation. It originates in the limited perspective of the isolated self, which means when we're judging, we're limiting our capacity to know what's real, and our perspective is not aligned with truth. Let's look at how it affects us and how it seems to serve us on some of the deepest levels.

When we judge ourselves and how we feel, we buy into the trip that we're in control of ourselves and our lives. Why? Because we judge as a way to understand, and when we judge ourselves, we believe we better understand ourselves, and so we feel more prepared for what may or may not happen. We do it all the time, especially around how we feel. For example, we take our emotional temperature. It reads "happy," and so we walk out the door feeling confident. And when the thermometer comes up "sad," "empty," or "bored," we mask and disguise that nakedness as a way to avoid being discovered as the sensitive, fluctuating creatures we are. Indeed, to reveal our vulnerability to others brings us into a realm of authenticity that can smash our ideas of ourselves into a thousand unrecognizable pieces, and thus leave us with no understanding of ourselves. So we choose to hide ourselves instead of revealing ourselves as we authentically are, opting for a no-risk path that is experienced as more familiar and predictable and not scary or disruptive of our plans.

Here again, everything we're doing is an effort to avoid losing who we are, losing our identity or our recognition of ourselves (i.e., "I'm not my normal self today"), and to avoid not being loved. Letting go of judgment is letting go of control and letting go of the possible understanding of who we thought we were.

Judging reduces things in a way that destroys our potential of knowing what they truly are, including ourselves. And, by the way, there's no such thing as your "normal" self, for we are all fluid beings, constantly changing and rebirthing as we dance with life.

Here is something worth considering: What would happen if, all of a sudden, you felt "strange," and instead of saying to yourself, "I feel strange. Something is wrong," you just allowed that moment to unfold, calling it nothing, just watching it as it passed? What if you stopped having good days and bad days and just had days? What if you stopped describing them and stopped obsessing over the details of how and why you feel what you feel?

Well, I'm going to tell you: By and by you would start realizing that *it all passes* and that life is always changing. You would realize it was never *what was happening* or *what you were feeling* that was so challenging; it was your judgment of it and your efforts to control life that made you suffer. It was your resistance to reality—your flying against the wind—that kept knocking you down. You would have space to get to what's *really* bothering you beneath it all. "Depression," "frustration," and "anxiety" would come to melt away with your letting go of the labels, with your allowing your experience to move and shift and morph and be wordless.

Sorting out your inner experience with self-judgment is huge, because, after all, it all begins and ends with you. If you're cool with yourself, you will be cool with others. If you're cruel to yourself, you will be cruel to others (even if only in your head). Whatever you do to yourself, you will do to the other, too. What this means is that as you resolve your self-judgment, so, too, will your judgment of others cease and fade.

Now, with the understanding that we are the point of origin for all that we experience, let's take a look at what happens to us when we fear the judgment of other people. After all, it can be helpful to look at it from a few different angles. When we monitor ourselves via our fear of others' judgments, we allow ourselves to be controlled by them. So if you do or don't do this or that because you're afraid of what others may think, say, or do, then you become controlled by your ideas about others' distortions. Really, you are controlling yourself, but you are doing it through the guise of the other. (Trippy, but true.)

If we are discussing judgment, then it is worth also discussing observation. Whereas judgment is when we decide that anything *is* this or that, observation is the objective process of noticing simply that which factually happens *without* then defining it. An observation, for example, could be, "He is screaming" or "I've been feeling a lot of sadness in my heart lately." What often happens, though, is that we then connect that factual observation with what *it means to us*, such as, "He is screaming, therefore, he's an angry jerk," or "I feel a lot of sadness in my heart lately, therefore, I must be depressed." From there, our subconscious mind connects even more dots, associating that once innocent observation with the things that we associate with sadness and anger, and even more interpretations and experiences are created from there.

Observation in and of itself is an integral aspect of intelligence. The thing to keep an eye on is how we define and decorate our observations with the associations we make, which often tells us a lot more about ourselves than the person or situation we are describing. We must remember that our lens of perception is often spotted, and that it is best to default to factual observations and interact with others and ourselves on that objective basis (and not our interpretation of it). Marshall Rosenberg has done tremendous work in this arena, and I encourage you to read his book *Nonviolent Communication* for a deeper understanding.

Judgment of another limits your potential experience with that person. For example, if you judge someone as being stupid, most likely that's what you're going to see because you're already focused on that. You won't be open, because judgment is naturally closed, and because of that, you will miss precious treasures. If you judge the person you are dating as not being enough *this* or being way too *that*, your perspective is contracted, and for as long as you believe these thoughts, you won't know whether or not there is actually magic between you two.

Life is about intimacy, and an intimacy with all of life, at that. This intimacy is a making love with life, and if we are to move into it more and more, we open to life beyond our ideas. As we move past our tendency to judge, refusing to stop there, and keep taking in the world beyond the frames, we become privy to the splendor of what is before us and the magic of what we already are.

We Are a Communion with God

What we are is a living, breathing communion with God, which means, even in a most extreme case, such as the committing of a murder, the Divine does not turn its back. It is simply impossible for *that which we are* to disappear, and what we are *is* the communion with God manifest in physical form. While committing a murder symbolizes that one is out of alignment with God, it does not correlate to unworthiness or disinheritance. God disinherits no one. In other words, we can behave in a way that is unholy, but that cannot invalidate that each of us is a child of God. Consider it: When people have absolutely nothing else to lose, what do they find? They find God. Because God is the only thing that cannot be lost.

One who is in touch with the God within could never do something like commit a murder, which is exactly why the act is considered unholy. Which is exactly why remembering our divinity is so important. It is the single most important part of our existence, for to do so creates a life of harmony for us and the world, and to not do so perpetuates the kaleidoscope of illusion, in which all things perceived are a reflection of one's own feeling of inadequacy, incompletion, loneliness, and separation from God. We don't need rules; we only need to remember our Selves.

And so all of this control and all of these rules are totally unnecessary and are nothing more than plastic ladder rungs on the fictitious playground of morality, spirituality, and religion, where one thinks the Oz of God will open a shiny door and say, "Wellllcome! You repeated your millionth mantra! Wellllcome! You killed in my name! Wellllcome! You never ate pork. Hel-looooo, my child!" But only in the realm of humans do we have stories like this.

God is simple—pure and simple. When you let go of the ideas, the rules, the self-labeling, the dramas, and settle into the sim-plicity of your being, into the *silence* of your being, the meeting begins. Then the room is the right temperature, the lighting is just nice enough, and the music is about to come on.

Don't Clip Your Wings

By letting go of control, you become vastly more capable of real-izing and embodying your potential. Letting go of control needs a certain relaxation, and when you are very relaxed, both your mind and your heart open up to such an extent that they are able to receive infinitely more information, sensation, wisdom, and so on. To control our feelings is to be in a state of tension. And holding on to feelings only allows them to stagnate. When we are repressing ourselves like that, we interfere with life's pro-cess, and an otherwise benign passing feeling becomes something negative or unsupportive. Interfering with our natural process in this way distorts our perception and shifts the reality we *intend* to create into something limited and strained. I like to think of my experience of life and all that unfolds through me and within me like this: I have no interest in getting too involved with it all. No, thank you—I'm staying out of it. That's for God.

If you actually had control over life, you would realize very quickly that you would not want it nor would you know what to do. That is an immense and a very boring responsibility—you would beg and plead for divine forces to take over. You cannot simultaneously live and have control over life. It is one or the other. Being dazzled by existence is much more sensational.

We have no idea what is going to happen. We have no idea when or how we will die, let alone how we will feel tomorrow or even tonight. And this is just the thing. Once you start falling in love with the free fall, you start to really live. Only when you jump do you realize you can fly and do you realize you had wings all along. Only in the free fall can you catch golden stars in your hair. Everything your soul longs for requires your release of control. You have not known the potential of love if you have remained in control. Same with sex. Same with art. Same with singing and cooking and a good walk along the river. It is true that control diminishes your ability to appreciate. If you cannot know something in its essence, you cannot fully appreciate it. And when you are in control, judging something, you cannot know it or get close to the truth of what it really is. You cannot be truly intimate with it or move into union. It's not possible because you are in division.

When you limit your perspective you limit your ability to love and to know. When you go into control, rules, judgment—when you distort and withhold your energy and you cannot share your love—you perish. You die a million little deaths; a million little fires get extinguished instead of touching both you and the world.

A life well lived is about being true to your Self in the moment, no matter what that may be. It's about getting messy, feeling into it, feeling the *depth* of it, expressing the mushy gushy of your heart, making love on the first date if that feels right, trusting your instinct to eat meat even though you haven't in ten years. It's about trusting your intuition and diving into the invitations that beckon you, even if they clash with your ideas about yourself. That is the only description of a life that honors, embodies, and supports your spiritual nature: *doing what you need to do to be in truth with your Self.* This is the hand that helps a thousand hands, the heart that touches a million hearts. When you get to the truth of *you*, we all get closer to home.

Chapter 9

ACCEPTING YOUR
DIVINE POWER

Our deepest fear is not that we are inadequate. Our deepest fear is
that we are powerful beyond measure. It is our light, not our darkness,
that most frightens us. We ask ourselves, Who am I to be brilliant,
gorgeous, talented, fabulous? Actually, who are you *not* to be? You are
a child of God. Your playing small doesn't serve the world.

MARIANNE WILLIAMSON, *A Return to Love*

Deep within us all is the divine principle that created the whole
universe. Contemplate that for a moment:

Deep within you
is the divine principle
that created the entire universe.

Take a moment to tune in to it and sense it. The implication
of this simple fact is that we are extraordinarily powerful beings.
If the same power that created the earth, the sky, the wonder of
rainbows and music and waterfalls, in fact, lives and breathes
within us, then we are home to a creative power and insight that
surpasses our wildest imaginations. We are the dwelling place
of God and the inexhaustible energy of existence that creates all

worlds within worlds—and either with or without knowing it, we manifest and create within our own lives every single moment.

The light that lives within us is the light of God. The isolated, identified self feels pale in comparison, and that is because *it is*. This is why we must *die if we want to live*: By letting the false self burn in the furnace of truth, we meet our true Self and the God within. The small, isolated self can never be handed the light of God. Rather, the isolated self dissolves in the light of God and the true power within. In other words, the isolated self *itself* can never know, experience, or be the divine power that our true Selves are.

As spiritual teacher and author Marianne Williamson suggests, our "playing small" by remaining in the isolated, identified states we often exist in does not serve the world. Pretending or believing we are not as wonderful and uniquely gifted as we are does not help anyone, least of all ourselves. To begin to get in touch with the profundity that dwells inside of us, it is helpful to take a closer look at the space between us and the divine power within.

Many of us fear the responsibility that comes along with knowing and holding our greatness. We fear it, up until a certain point, because we don't trust ourselves. Rather, we fear ourselves, and we fear ourselves because we fear our minds. And as we have explored in great detail, until we have learned the ways of the mind and made friends with it, indeed, the mind can influence our behavior. And as long as we allow the mind to control our behavior, we are right to be afraid.

To work through this fear, it helps to become aware of what we mistakenly thought power was, then to learn what power really is, and from there to unearth the remembrance of what it feels like to relax into the power within.

Power Defined

In general, when we think of power, one of two things comes to mind. One is the material/egoic version of power, the type of power that is believed to be available to *some* but not *all*. Here, power is something that is exerted and projected through action/doing. Usually, there is a status attached to wealth, fame, notoriety, or some sort of high standing within society; for example, a person with a voice that others will obey, that others will follow. And all this is really an *idea* of power that has been totally perverted. It is a corrupt, out-of-control idea that billions of people have bought into. It is the standard he-who-has-the-money-has-the-power power. This sort of "power" usually keeps people up at night in an exhausting attempt at maintaining and increasing that power, while they neglect the spiritual nature of themselves, life, and love.

The other version of power is the real power. It is the one we sense in different leaders, teachers, children, or even a particularly radiant stranger. It is their shine. Their presence. Their authenticity. Their calmness and ease. Their incredible ability to share that which is true to them with a grace that is inspiring. The way in which they allow themselves to speak from their heart, even when doing so is challenging. We notice how easy it is to listen to them and how so many others are listening to them, too. How they are touched by a sort of deep wisdom. It is the power of the person who is totally him- or herself—his or her true Self.

These inspiring people are simply allowing themselves to be the channels of divinity they are designed to be. They have gotten out of their own way enough to let their divinity shine through. True power is unconditional and impersonal. It is nothing that can be devised or constructed; it can only be allowed. The destructive version of power, on the other hand, can only be built, achieved, and obtained, and therefore is both conditional and seemingly personal. It is completely *outside* of oneself and is always future oriented. When you die, it dies. And it's fear-based because it's caked in control, whereas true power is simply the overflow of love. Indeed, true power is *inner*, is beyond the constructs of the mind, is eternal, and exists in the now. Corrupt power is not actually power at all but an illusion humans have created to feel that their lives are meaningful and valid. It is a product of both an unhealthy relationship with the ego and not knowing the truth within.

At its core, the unhealthy version of power satisfies nothing more than egoic pleasures, which are fleeting and ultimately depleting. The more we indulge in this power, the more we move away from our center and our truth. This is fact.

Many people go through their entire lives staying at a level of illusion and unconsciousness. They swing from pleasure to pain, and ultimately, something deep within is being neglected. For some people, to live like this is enough, and that is fine. He who is happy in his dream—let him be. That is his journey. We can all only do the work ourselves.

Divine Power

As we go into a deeper meditative state of living, and as we allow ourselves to be channels of divine movement and divine inspiration, we begin to meet the power that lives within. Within each one of us is an Aladdin's cave, a treasure chest of glorious, infinite bounty. The more we commit to living life from a meditative state, which is greatly supported by having a daily meditation practice, the more these subtle energies reveal themselves to us. This power is that which literally *turns us on*. This power is the *ultimate* turn-on; it is the high others are trying to find through sex and drugs and get momentary glimpses of, at only a fraction of its potential.

To be magnetic for the life that emanates from your essence as your true vision, that is power. In other words, to naturally attract and manifest the life that matches your divine, most true frequency and most fulfilling possibility, simply because you exist, that's where it's at. And that natural attraction of the most fulfilling version of your life is what happens as you integrate into the Self. That is what you are seeing within the teachers, artists, and other beings who turn you on, who effortlessly, even wordlessly, inspire you to remember the truth of God and of who you are. What you are seeing within them is simply divine truth in action, and seeing it within another reflects it directly back to you, so that it resonates with the deepest part of you, reminding you of the divinity that rests within you, too.

True power includes being turned on to divinity. The Divine is brilliant beyond our wildest imagination, and when we finally give up and surrender to the flow of the Divine within us, incredible things begin to happen. Then we really get to know the extent of what is possible in life. Only when we hand over to God the box of ideas and images we have so carefully curated throughout our lives can we finally get a taste of what is real. Only then can God smash that well-disguised prison box into the dazzling black glitter of mystery it always was—and only then will you discover that within that dazzling black glitter live the untold love songs of a thousand years of your heart. These are the ultimate love songs, and they can only be discovered by you when you stop knowing so much—when you know nothing. When the atmosphere within becomes like that—when you're floating in the black glitter and trusting the mystery—you are letting yourself become a magic wand of existence, and you get to discover how unimaginably blissful, creative, and synchronistic life really is.

Children have this power. To even begin to invite your playful, childlike nature to return is a step. Never underestimate the power of invitation. To just breathe deeply and notice your surroundings, to allow it to fulfill your being with pleasure and satisfaction, that is a step. To look up from the sandwich that you are eating at the café and quietly notice the other people around you, the sound of the fork hitting the plate, the sound of the child crying—to notice and feel all of this without narration, while simultaneously feeling your breath, feeling the energy within your body—that is a step, a huge step. All of this is a mysterious remembering and a reawakening of the power within.

How Do We Get There?

The fear of your power is related to the fear of your mind, and the fear of losing your mind is the fear of going crazy and losing control. The distinction to be aware of is that the fear is of the craziness of the mind, though, and not of yourself. The fear is not of your true power.

When you know the power within, it becomes impossible to fear that things could go in some insane, out-of-touch-with-reality way, because the opposite happens. With our wild blossoming comes the fruition of our true minds, our true Selves, and the free-flow of our deepest, most inherent nature: divine power. The power we can trust. The power we can relax into. The power that takes care of itself.

When we let go of our conditioning, our beliefs, and our ideas about the way things *should* be, we are letting go of certain limiting constructs of the mind. The more and more we let go of "our" mind, the more and more we get in touch with *the true mind*—the total mind, which includes both the conscious mind and the great subconscious mind we all share, of which there is only one and that we are connected to at all times. Through the spaciousness we create through our steadfast retraining and deconstruction, domination ends, clarity arrives, and it becomes increasingly simple to employ the mechanism of the mind as a friend and a tool. From this space it also becomes increasingly easier to tune in to the true mind, the mind that is touched and influenced by divine thoughts and intuition. It's the cleansed mind in optimal relationship to the rest of our being.

The true mind is a timeless zone of psychic nature and great wisdom and all else that can exist or be translated into thought form. When we tune in to "our" subconscious, we are really tuning in to the aspect of the great one subconscious that resonates with us.

So the more we retrain our energy by moving it out of the head and into the heart, and the more we reorient our awareness to the present moment and anchor within it, the more the power of truth can begin to direct our lives, and the more we can work with the great subconscious mind to our betterment and not our detriment. And from there we can begin to realize the true mind for the treasure chest it is. We can work with the divine power within to weed out and resolve that which is resonating in our experience that does not serve us, that which pulls us out of alignment with our truest vision, like old memories and self-limiting beliefs, such as, "I can't do this" (in reference to "doing what we need to do" to follow the divine vision of our lives that inspires us and lights us up).

This work is very subtle, but all that is needed is the meditative state of our being and the knowingness that it is possible. For example, by simply "giving it back to God" (which we will discuss in depth in an upcoming chapter), we can offer back up the limiting beliefs and wounds for liberation and transmutation.

We can also call in the beliefs and understandings that serve us and resonate as our truth, such as, "I know I am supported in creating the highest vision of my life."

In other moments, the work is more direct. Oftentimes, in order to liberate the pain, trauma, and misinformed ideas we have about ourselves, we must reflect on the past and re-enter the inner scene of those memories. There are many ways we can work through the misunderstandings, confusion, and pain, but for the sake of our discussion the point is that we *can*, indeed, work through them. We are not tethered to the pain inside, even though it may absolutely feel like that. With our patience, acceptance, accountability, and acknowledgment of our divine power, we can move mountains both alone and with the support of others, when needed.

By taking care of ourselves in this way and ever moving toward the direction of cleansing the mirror and purifying the channels that we are, we begin to settle more into our true Selves. And when we settle more into our true Selves, we settle more into our power.

Our Perspective Is Our Power

As mentioned, we are always actively creating our lives (whether we are aware of it or not), and this is exactly why we so deeply fear our power. Somehow, we sense that we are unspeakably powerful creators of our reality, and we do not trust ourselves with this responsibility. The massive accountability we all have for our lives can seem truly daunting when we realize it for the first time. For this reason, when we brush up against our power, one of two things typically happens: either the fear takes over and we remain unconscious, or we consciously try to fix or heal ourselves so we can one day create the life we desire.

The direction to go, however, is into Divine Perspective. The Divine Perspective tells us we do not need to be healed and that nothing within us needs to be fixed. It tells us that the root of any problem is our perspective, the way we are looking at it. It tells us that by changing our perspective, we change our lives, and that by aligning with the Divine Perspective, we align our vision with God's. The root of all fear and suffering is a distorted perspective, and those "problems" are transformed as our perspective aligns with the Divine Perspective.

As you begin to resolve old traumas and areas where you have shut yourself down, you may feel the need to consult different practitioners and explore different techniques for "healing." Self-healing can include some very powerful work (profoundly transformative work, in fact, and work that is vital if we are to brave the journey within for cleansing and liberation), but the key is to stay tuned for the moment when you realize that you are not being healed. Things are being released, yes. Energy is changing, yes. But what is actually happening? Energy is being transformed and perspective is shifting, and as a result, you feel different. But did you, the *truth* of you, ever once change?

This realization is another gateway to realizing the nature of our being. It is another doorway to the infinite well of starry mud and oneness that rests within us. It is the moment we begin to realize that *all is well*. It was just that some heavy baggage was festering, and it did not belong there anymore. But we were always inherently well and remain well. It's in this realizing that we start to resonate with something more true. And when we allow this recognition, this resonance, and this vibration to recalibrate our perspective, many things begin to change on their own.

Until the moment we begin to move into this alignment, it's fair enough that we are afraid. Until we have a good grip on what's floating around in our subconscious mind and what's influencing our reality and our perspective, coming into our power can indeed be a destructive thing. Why? Because then the truth of us is not directing the show. Because then we're in *ego power* and not *divine power*. Until we have a solid understanding of how the mechanism works, and until we can mostly distinguish the real from the unreal, it's not possible to enter our divine power. Until we are sharing from our inner truth, the source of our sharing is not pure.

So, it is totally reasonable and justified to be afraid of it up until that point of awareness. And we can either jump into truth from the cliff of blindness, with a true finger on its pulse, in mysterious, undeniable recognition, or we can jump from the cliff of vision, having already cleared out enough weeds and recovered the sense that it is safe. Wherever we jump from does not matter. What matters is that our finger is on the pulse of truth, that we are always in connection with that recognizable pulse, the totally undeniable, silent rhythm of that which is indestructible, real, vital, immortal, and true—and that when we are sure we can't recognize it, we trust that we can and let that trust become a lifeline. I cannot encourage us all enough to cultivate a daily meditation practice as a way of staying in recognition of this pulse.

The more we go into that bloodline, the more the divine power can move us, can guide us. Keeping one eye firmly focused upon that pulse at all times is like handing over the microphone to the divine power within. From there, all we need to do is listen.

The Power of Choice

Over and over again, that which we discuss is embodied and enlivened through our power of choice. This power is paramount in our lives, directs all, chooses war or peace, suffering or acceptance. Our power of choice is our unconditional, ever-present opportunity for integration, embodiment, and empowerment. Our power comes to life through the choices we make. And the presence of our power is strengthened when reflected through the consistency of our decisions—decisions that *support* us. Indeed, it is our fate to decide where we place our attention and what we therefore birth into life.

When you make a decision, you kill off other possibilities. If you choose *this*, then you kill off *that*. That is the etymology of the word *decision*. In Latin, *decider* means "to decide, to determine, and to cut off"—to eliminate the other possibilities. Here, we are talking about your decision to be alert and aware. Your decision to be turned on and vigilant, and to be compassionate and relaxed with yourself when you are not. Your decision to work with the present moment as an opportunity. Your decision to keep the Divine Perspective of *all is well*, even if that means learning it through the practice of it and through being compassionate toward yourself for not yet truly knowing it. Or even trusting all is well behind the intensity of the breakdown, behind the fury of misunderstanding and confusion of whatever is happening. It is your choice to commit to releasing the interpretation of anything as a "problem" and instead bow down over and over again at the heels of this mysterious, benevolent life.

The choice to surrender our perspective to the Divine Perspective is a gift that keeps giving. The *ultimate* gift that keeps giving. Through it, we realize our power is rooted in our non-reactivity, maintained through our relaxed watchfulness, and engaged through our choices. And we choose love. We choose to work with the ingredients of life as they present themselves to us, rather than being controlled by them or moved by fear. We choose to stay present as we move into ever-widening clarity.

When we decide to make choices that feed us, nurture us, and carry us home, we move more deeply into our Selves. This is the way of the shining light. Coincidentally, it is also the path of service. To make these choices is to create the best possibilities for our lives and enable us to share our love in the most wonderful of ways. It is to move into the great giving, loving ceremony of life in its most divine, enjoyable, meaningful possibility.

Chapter 10

MOVING INTO MYSTERY
AND TRUST

If you can trust, something or other will always happen and will
help your growth. You will be provided for. Whatsoever is needed
at a particular time will be given to you, never before it. You get
it only when you need it, and there is not even a single moment's
delay. When you need it you get it, immediately, instantly!
That's the beauty of trust. By and by you learn the ways of how
existence goes on providing for you, how existence goes on caring
about you. You are not living in an indifferent existence. It does
not ignore you. You are unnecessarily worried; all is provided for.
Once you have learnt the knack of trust, all worry disappears.

OSHO, *The Wisdom of the Sands,* Vol. 2, Talk #1

"Once you have learnt the knack of trust," says Osho, "all worry
disappears." Trust is a trump card, a divine rod of faith that
penetrates all uncertainty, transforming it back into love. It's the
knowingness of what is, that *you are taken care of*, and it is a faith
that boomerangs. The more you melt into trust, the more you
see and experience how infinitely provided for you are. And the
more you witness that, the more you experience it.

Trust includes the understanding that whatever is happening is an offering for your growth and evolution. It is an

understanding of love, for love can never hurt you. You can be hurt by your attachment or your expectations, yes, but love itself can never hurt you.

And deeper so, trust is the silent language, the bedrock that makes you fertile and sharp for the revelation of every moment's gift. Where there is trust, life is seen for the divine unfolding it is, and all happenings, all surprises, all moments are witnessed with an energy that dissolves the questions. Where there is trust, there is a blossoming of life. This state of being can begin as a position you take or a decision you make, as you begin to learn it and know it more cellularly, more deeply. It can start out like that until it becomes part of your very being, a fluency that becomes your way.

As Osho specified, trust is something that can indeed be learned. Through your focus and intelligence, you can tune in to it. Learning to trust is like learning to play an instrument: it takes practice, precision, and attention, and it takes an awareness and respect for the subtleties. It takes a humbleness to sit quietly enough, carefully enough, to hear what is being said in its significance, to know you cannot dominate it, to know you can only allow yourself to learn.

We cannot talk about trust without talking about doubt. Let's differentiate between true doubt and what I like to call artificial doubt. True doubt is a healthy, supportive part of the human experience. It is a sacred shadow aspect through which we may discover what we truly desire and what we truly are. It helps us discern what is true from what is not. Artificial doubt, on the other hand, is that sort of lazy overuse of words or indulgence in the mind when something is not going your way and you find yourself getting a bit heavy on the "oh, this sucks" or the "oh, it's not going to work out." It's that whiny, shallow perspective. And all it does is delay you; it just puts you a step farther away from whatever is in the midst of being created. It's sloppy. It means you are not really paying attention. In short, artificial doubt is nothing more than a bad habit to quit, and true doubt is a pure refrain of life that helps to show you what is real.

We also cannot talk about trust without acknowledging its deep relationship with mystery. Trust dances directly with mystery, for mystery lives in the very heart of trust and trust in the very heart of mystery. We trust in totality when we have given ourselves over to the mystery of life. Through inviting life to show us what it has in store for us, we release ourselves into the sea of possibilities, which may raise us up and pull us down through the waves of moments on the way to the shore of our vision manifest. The way there is not for us to decide; it is for God to reveal, for God to align and keep aligning us with the ever-changing, transforming symphony of life. Only through this trust and total surrender to the mystery can we tap into the sweetest of all possibilities for our lives.

Only through the heart of trust can you get closer to the mystery. (You can also get closer to trust through the mystery, but that might be a wilder ride.) Trust is needed for this courtship, which is perhaps the most divine, illustrious courtship in this life. To know the mystery and to be one with it is to know life. It is to know the sultry, begging-on-your-knees-that-you-cannot-take-any-more beauty, for if you do, you will explode. It is the ultimate tantric union.

Diving into the mystery can be scary at first, but once you experience its miraculousness, you come to know a profound poetry of life, and you never go back. To be sure, to give yourself over to the great mystery of life is to know a sensuality beyond any other. It is a flirtation that leads to the sweetest of deaths and the brightest of births. Only through this intimacy with the mystery can you know the depth of what it means to be a lover and what it means to make love with life.

Life is a wise old woman. And if you know what is good for you, you know to never try to tell an old crone what to do. She knows how to work her magic just fine. She has been there and back a thousand times, and she has been paying attention all the way.

So do you really have the chutzpah, the arrogance, to say things should be any different than the way they are? And if you do, do you absolutely, truly believe yourself? And can anything other than your mind make such a statement? Can you really have that omniscience to say, above all divine energy, "Hey, God, what just happened should have happened differently"? Or can you see that you have the invitation to work with this moment as an opportunity? Or perhaps how you have attracted this moment to learn something?

"Divine Source, you got this one wrong." How can the energy that created you be wrong, and yet you be right? It is not possible. You are that. Imagine you have written a song and then the song says, "Oh dear, this is all wrong. The bass really needs to fade out at the end. I should have a D sharp where I have a C minor. I need Taylor Swift on vocals." The song would be crazy! It came from you, it is a piece of you, and yet it asserts that *your inspiration* to birth the song is not on track, only its inspiration is. Talk about a real Frankenstein situation. But alas, the song will always be the simple beauty that is the song. It can only surrender to the grace of your inspiration to play it. So just be like the song, and tune in to yourself as a song of God within a much larger divine symphony.

Through this way of being, a greater possibility reveals itself and an infinite gratitude emerges. You become grateful for the guy or girl who stood you up for dinner (for he/she was obviously not "the one"), grateful for the sprained ankle that forced you to slow down for the day. Grateful for the way the rain poured all over your new sweater because, hey, you almost got angry, but instead, you chose to feel the radiance of being alive. You start seeing the way in which you attract things into your life as opportunities to learn and remember, and you become more fine-tuned to discover what they are telling you. Remember, life is totally and completely unpredictable, and if it becomes predictable, then something is stale.

Life is inherently benevolent and takes nothing away without bringing you that which is more aligned. Your trust in the benevolent nature of existence is what keeps the song going in the most magical way for you. No intriguing song is filled with only high notes. Rather, really good, profound songs have depth, dimension, and a shifting flow of notes. So, too, the song of life is a divine flow of moments—sacred moments that give depth and dimension to the ceremony. Knowing this will help you soar in the sky of unconditional magic.

Trust Begets Patience

Trust begets patience. Often, we feel ready for something, and yet still it does not arrive. True trust is total, and even in moments of impatience and doubt, it is there to remind us that we know nothing. We may feel ready, we may think we are ready (and hey, perhaps we are), but the whole picture is not ready to manifest yet. Perhaps the other side of the vision is still getting ready to meet us. Whatever the reason for the perceived delay, it is not for us to understand or to know; it is just for us to trust. All comes in its moment.

The trust, the mystery, is always there, welcoming your arrival. Just take a fine, quiet look at life and be willing to see its synchronistic goodness. Discover it all from within, and look outside from the stillness within. Only in your unwillingness can you miss it.

The sun comes up every day. Even in unwillingness, you cannot deny that. Would you say that you trust it will rise again tomorrow, or would you simply say that it comes up—no trust needed? "No trust needed" is the embodiment of trust, for in your union with it, trust becomes a fluent part of your being. It is no longer a concept; it is just a vibration of your being—a fact of life. The sun will rise, the seasons will change, life will be born and change and die and be born again. On and on, life goes on cycling and purifying and taking care of itself. It is our union with trust that nurtures our flow with the generous, providing nature of life where everything—by virtue of being divine—continually takes care of itself.

Challenging feelings will move and shift, and if you are very present with them and if you are in trust, the movement will be a dance and that dance will be beautiful, even when it is ugly. If you are in trust during the most challenging moments of life—if you *are* trust—a very deep, profound poetry is revealed. You let yourself burn in the furnace of truth, knowing that which is real will always remain, and through the deaths of different parts of you and different parts of your life, a great transformation takes place. This is the promise of life; this is the ceremony.

Trust This Moment

Ultimately, we can only know and trust this moment and wherever life takes us from here. Projecting this moment into the future can be supportive and important at times (for after all, this projection is a v*ital aspect of manifestation and creation*). However, when we depend on anything turning out a certain way or believe that it must turn out that way, we are deluding ourselves. When we buy into expectations and ideas about life and what *should* happen, and they then don't come to fruition as we had wished or planned, we often feel disappointed—but not because of trust. Not because life or anyone has done anything wrong. Rather, we suffer in those moments because of our perspective, our expectations, and our attachments to beliefs, people, and so on.

It is so much easier to give it all back to God and let life take over, and this is a key to living the expanse of life as the spiritual practice. Ultimately, if it's us against life, life will win every single time. So better to find our way onto the same team as life, which we have always been on anyway. Better to relax into the wild home of it all.

We must remember that we can only simply trust, and not any one thing. It can only ever be for *all of life*. The only thing to know is *yes, God*. When there is trust, it is pervasive. It is for all, for everything, without exclusion, and it allows the bigger picture to come into existence in its best way for us.

A couple of years ago, something happened in my life that deeply challenged my sense of trust. After spending much time traveling, my beloved and I had chosen to try living in Australia, where he's from, to see if it was meant to be our home base. I was there with him on an American tourist visa, which meant I could only be there for three months at a time. After spending my first three months there, I traveled to Bali, where I stayed for six weeks before heading back to Australia.

While I was in Bali, my love found us a home, bought us a car, and began working. After so much time traveling, we had been feeling, "Ah, finally, we can rest, settle down, and grow some roots." We had a beautiful vision sorted: He would go on a ten-day vipassana meditation retreat during my final days in Bali. Upon returning to Australia, I would head straight to our new home and fill it with love for us both. He would return a couple days after me, I would welcome him into our new home, and we would be reunited, both rested and renewed and ready to begin this new chapter together.

What actually happened, though, was that I was deported from Australia immediately upon arriving. An immigration official decided I was violating the terms of my visa, sent me to a detention center, and a day later, I was on a plane back to the United States.

It was intense to feel blindsided by life, and for a long moment while in the detention center, the confusion and doubt that swelled had me wondering if I really could trust life to just take care of me. But after I'd had a few good cries, it became clear that life just had other plans for us. Better, more aligned plans, to be sure. It sent us into another year of travel, which by then we had grown weary of but were grateful for nonetheless, and in each moment, we stepped more and more into deeper alignment with the callings of our lives. Through this great shift that life had pushed us into, we both began expressing and stepping into our gifts more and more. During our travels, this book was birthed, I was magically and unexpectedly offered representation by my wonderful agent, and I signed a contract with an amazing publisher. And shortly thereafter, we found our home, got married, and watched this abundance and good flow begin to manifest financially, too. All in one year.

Sorting out this little kink in our perspective—*that trust could ever be something conditional that we decide and we project*—is very helpful in realigning with the magic of its current. We must keep relaxing deeper into trust if we are to keep seeing things from the Divine Perspective and integrating into the powerful Creators we all are.

It Will Be So

Trust is a meditation with life itself. It is a meditation on the movement of life. It is giving yourself up to the stars, letting yourself go to be pulled into the rhythm of it all. It is closing your eyes and saying to life, "Take me, I'm yours. I know you've got me. I know you're listening to me. Yes, have your way with me." And if you are saying that to life, then you are saying that to God. What you start to realize is that life is God, and God is life. Life is love, and love is life. And you, you are all of that. So let life take over.

Chapter 11

EMOTIONS, FEELINGS, AND LEARNING HOW TO SUFFER WELL

Awakening is not about deleting or transcending human emotions, for how would the ocean transcend a single wave, and how would the sun transcend one of its beloved sunbeams? It's about seeing that every emotion—from joy to despair, bliss to boredom, agony to ecstasy—is only a movement of life energy, actually a movement of yourself, a wave in your vastness. No emotion is a threat, an enemy, or a punishment.

JEFF FOSTER, author of *The Deepest Acceptance*,
social media update, March 9, 2015

To embody our potential and align with the Divine could never mean we transcend all emotion and *om* our way through life. Rather, it means we welcome all that comes up in the wild scheme of emotions and feelings. More so, it means that we really go for it—really welcome it, really feel it, and really learn from it. *Omming* our way out of intolerable pain or anger or a breakdown or convincing ourselves to just "focus on the light" (give it no attention) is just a well-disguised form of escapism, and anyway, it does not work. While it is implicit that we focus on that which we wish to enhance, the only thing repression, avoidance, or spiritualizing ourselves out of our emotions does is inspire us to feel separate from the good flow of life.

Think back to our discussion on control: the moment we begin to say no, the flow of our connection gets cramped. And while sometimes saying no to something is saying yes to that which is entirely more aligned for us, all other no's are just tourniquets in the flow of life. Every joy and every pain is welcome in the immense play of life, where everything is the clay of love, revealing the endless textures and forms we can experience.

When we live like the brilliant stars we are, we welcome all that arises, and we do so from a watchful space, unattached and nonreactive. Consider it: the very stars above us do little more than watch, sparkling as they accept the moment of their falling and implosion with as much grace and power as their burst into existence. As they hang electric in space, they watch all that happens, embodying and responding only to the buzz of existence within both themselves and the universe of which they are a part.

As we become more and more watchful, we become more like a star. The seesaw of life's experiences, feelings, and emotions can then be witnessed, embraced, and experienced from higher up on the pendulum—which is to say, the swings will become less and less dramatic. At first, when we become aware, the constantly changing energy of our lives and ourselves can feel very intense. (Is it more intense than it was before? Often not; rather, with our increased awareness comes our increased sensitivity and noticing of that which we hadn't noticed before.) With the deepening of our inner meditation comes the shrinking distance of those swings, and with that, the seesaw can be more easily seen and loved for the divine play of polarity it is. From here we can laugh at ourselves, appreciating our shadows and embracing where we still are learning with the same love and understanding we give to a child, for we are all children of this universe, no matter how old or wise. From here we can begin to understand and laugh with the great cosmic joke.

To be totally alive means to be touched by life. It means to answer the phone every time life calls. So when sadness knocks on the door, we open it, for to keep it closed is to say no to life and is to sentence sadness to a life of exile, rotting at the doorstep of our heart, filling us with a stinking perfumery that does nothing good for the soul.

In accepting all, we accept unconditionally that which arises within. And as mentioned, it is only then that we move into acceptance of that which arises in others. Now, let me be clear: to accept that which arises in others does not mean to withstand abusive behavior; rather, it means that we accept that this is what is happening within them as *their* life journey, *their* perspective, and we accept that we have the power and the choice to stay, to go, to have firm boundaries. Inviting anything into our lives *via our acceptance* is one of the most powerful ways we dialogue with God and create our realities. Acceptance of that which is within leads to inner peace. Acceptance of others' abusive behavior leads to destruction; acceptance of your power to leave abuse leads to peace.

To learn how to manage the more challenging emotions and feelings that arise, we must first remember over and over again that in the grand ceremony of life, all is welcome. By dissolving any resistance through the presence of our accepting nature, we take the first step. From there, no matter how hard it is (and boy, can it be hard sometimes), we must remember that nothing is personal. As extremely personal as things can seem, everyone is ultimately dealing with their own journeys and truths. I love how Miguel Ruiz explained this sentiment in *The Four Agreements*: "[I]t is not what I am saying that is hurting you; it is that you have wounds that I touch by what I have said. You are hurting yourself. There is no way that I can take this personally."

We must remember that wherever we are sensitive, whatever triggers us is a huge invitation to see what is inside, underneath. The bigger the reaction, the bigger the potential for freedom that rests beneath. (But sometimes even small reactions pave the way to great freedom, too.) So these are our two big steps: acceptance and looking inward to see what we are trying to learn, where we need to grow, what needs to release, or just giving ourselves love. Sometimes nurturance is the only thing needed.

It is important to sense whether or not it is best for us to dig through what's happening to discover what we are trying to learn, because what is best for us can change from moment to moment. Sometimes, this digging work is the last thing we need. Sometimes, we just need to wild out with the river and completely lose it. We must honor what is best for us in each new moment and situation, whether it's digging work to discover the teaching or simply being taken by the waves.

Remember the Guns N' Roses analogy regarding the influence of thoughts and how they relate to how we feel? In emotional moments, forms and figures, feelings and thoughts present themselves, and we choose that which we interact with. We choose *how* we interact with it. In other words, perhaps we notice that in a moment of hopelessness, the thought "It's never going to work out" surfaces. If it does, we see it, we recognize what is happening within us, and we choose to not get on that train of thought. We choose to carry on as we were or to move our body or to dance—to do whatever we need to do—as we sentiently honor that which is lodged within us, that which is coming to pass. We learn from it, and we move on.

We are forgiving with ourselves when we slip, for our very beings are made of forgiveness itself. The dance of life goes on, and life responds to us in its cyclical way. A divine dialogue has been created. We continue to receive that which we focus upon, and trust leads the way, raising that which we focus upon to its highest, most pure version. All for the sweet illumination of our life. And on and on the ceremony goes.

The ceremony may be filled with tears, with high-pitched screams of "Why?," and all that really means is that we are alive and astute. The stronger the tears, the stronger the movement. We must cry deep and hard to the absolute core of the feeling—we must cry in totality. Only then can we laugh and love in totality. We can only accept joy and laughter and experience them in their potential to the extent that we have accepted the other polarities of existence, like sadness and pain, in fullness and totality as well.

Totality is, of course, total, which means it is nonexclusive and says yes to all. If you are shouldering sadness, then you are shouldering love and joy. When you shoulder aside any one thing (or nudge it away), you shoulder aside the next thing, too, by nature of the laws of existence. When you shoulder aside sadness, something within you remains closed that would otherwise open with your full acceptance and experience. And that little bit that remains closed is a place where the laugher and joy that come cannot enter. They may have arrived, but they cannot soak into those spaces. So do all with totality. Only then are you living in fullness and knowing the potential of life.

Learning How to Suffer Well

To know the potential of life, we must learn how to suffer well. For that learning is based in acceptance, and as we have said, only through accepting all can we know the fullness and magic of life. In the messy buffet of different things we can feel in this life, we don't get to choose what is put onto our plate. We get to choose how we handle it, yes, but we do not choose the emotions that come. So if pain, as grief, frustration, heartbreak, and sadness, is on the divine menu, then we'd better get our nutrition and our digestive systems in order so we know how to assimilate them.

Suffering results from *how* we deal with that which comes; it's not the inherent experience itself. Most of us are born into the paradigm of suffering, and so we accept suffering as part of life. However, no one is doomed to suffer. We suffer only until we learn how to suffer well, and it is through that great learning that the paradigm of suffering is broken. Indeed, it is actually through the experience of suffering that we often come to realize that *we don't have to suffer when we experience pain.*

We are often inspired to suffer when our subjective truth falls out of alignment with objective, cosmic truth. In other words, suffering comes when we resist that which is happening and when we believe that which is happening *shouldn't* be happening, and that it's therefore a problem. As discussed, it is the attempts to deny and control reality and emotions that create the experience of suffering—which is to say, it is the strain of our own reins that hurts us.

When we let the song of what's happening take over and move through us, and remain only as the full-feeling witness, it has space to transform and shift as it most naturally is meant to. Otherwise, when we are trying to control our feelings and emotions, the CD starts to skip, and the chorus keeps repeating. The song, the natural shifting and cycling, becomes tainted, and the pain increases and suffering worsens exponentially. What might have lasted ten minutes gets stretched into ten days, or ten months, or ten years. It is a soul strangle, where your mind is ordering your hands to manipulate an otherwise ephemeral and divine experience.

So, how do you suffer well?

First of all, you must honor what is happening and any release that may be needed. Suffering happens when we fight off parts of life and parts of ourselves, and our journey through it is our journey back to ourselves. So begin by embodying your acceptance of how you feel (which may feel like the last thing you want to do). Cry, write, sing, meditate, scream, rage if you need to (in a safe place and in a safe way). Go for it *without* identifying with it. Connect with that place within you where the pain is. Remember, you are not that which passes; you are that which watches, that which is infinite and invincible. Honor that a paramount moment is happening within and that it deserves your attention, your permission, and your presence. Your permission may include releasing the need for answers (including to questions such as "Why is this happening?") when you're being taken by the river of experience. Release any need for clarity or understanding.

Next, don't judge what is happening. In the presence of pain, confusion, and so on, only by going *through* it can you become integrated and be propelled into vastness. Don't buy into the evaluation your mind offers you about what's happening, like believing it's a *problem*, that it *shouldn't* be happening, or that it's *wrong*. Likewise, don't buy into any of the labels that your mind suggests you give to yourself, like *crazy, insane, losing your mind, fucked up,* or *a total mess*. Believing the destructive ideas that the mind presents only energizes the suffering to spiral. The truth is that by traveling through the discomfort and letting out any "mess," you become clean; avoiding it or keeping it in is always at the expense of your clarity and freedom. Very few people are spared from getting messy—it is a consequence of being alive—so just let out whatever needs to be let out and take the pressure off, which is to say, don't take it too seriously. Even though they feel (and *are*) incredibly powerful and strong, these experiences are really no biggies in the sense that they are normal consequences of being alive, and we all go through it.

Once the big release has happened and you are feeling more quiet, or if releasing is not part of this moment for you, expand your perspective. Move your attention to the present world around you while simultaneously witnessing and feeling what is happening within. Choose to feel the pain and, at the same time, see beyond the pain. Remember the world outside. Go to the beach and watch the ocean, sit beside a tree and watch the grass, or lay beside a river as you honor, feel, and listen to the pain within.

Throughout it all, go through what you're going through without being overly self-involved. Fewer details, fewer words, less calling your closest friends to share stories and solicit advice. It is revolutionary to hold what you're going through sacredly with yourself and explore what happens. (Of course, when you feel you need support, then trust and follow that need, too.) Try it: Next time pain (or suffering) comes, allow whatever expression, release, or movement that rises to happen, and then go outside and look at the night sky. Stay present with what's happening within, and at the same time, watch the marvelous stars. Let them silently remind you. Or watch the waves of the ocean or the grass blowing in the wind. Go wherever you like, and give the releasing energy back to God and the earth (the practice of which we will discuss in more detail soon). And always, always do your best to discover what you are learning, *when it is the moment for that.* Pain can only exist within you if it has something to teach you. So connect with it and find out what it wishes to impart.

You could, of course, bitch and moan and wish that life were different, and wish that you could control your life, and experience only the highs and the ups, and no one can stop you. If that is your thing, okay. If that is what you've got to do, then *really* do it—really go for it and feel it. Because at the end of that road, life doesn't say to you, "Hey, okay, you can have control. You've suffered enough—hung in there enough. The jig is up. You can have control now, and everything will just be easy peasy for you from now on." That has never happened, not once in the history of humankind.

And so, what we realize is that learning how to suffer well is the oar that keeps us rowing our canoe through the night. When you meditate through the wild, painful moments, the moments so far beyond comprehension, and become open to the possibility that there is still beauty before you, you begin to touch a new gold and a new depth within. Through this meditation, you know both yourself and life more intimately.

When you meditate through life like this, you are in a constant state of growth, and your grace and your eminence flow through you and shine. You are living as the marvelous creature of God that you are, a golden child waving in the wind, letting yourself just be a song, like the beautiful harmony of the leaves in the wildest of windstorms. Could you imagine a windstorm without the rustling of the leaves? It would be strange, dead; something would be very unnatural. You are made of the same stuff as the leaves—and the wind. You are meant to be rustled and sung.

When we learn how to suffer well, we will find that the suffering miraculously stops, because the very thing that kept the suffering there in the first place has disappeared. The reflection changes, the paradigm shifts. The energy of illusion becomes diffused, for it cannot be upheld in the face of truth. So with the deepening of our surrender comes the burning of the ropes that bound us. The environment in which suffering thrives now dissolves, and the mechanisms utilized to perpetuate it become a technology so outdated that they just stop working. Indeed, suffering can only function when we believe any part of us or our life is separate from the Divine, and as we drop into the softness of acceptance, we once again become whole.

Often, through the most challenging events of our lives we experience tremendous, illuminating growth, and so moments spent in suffering have not been for naught. Suffering is filled with pressure and tension, and it can break us, and through a great breaking, the light of remembrance can enter. Restriction, constriction, and control can be so tight that we crack open in a supreme helplessness that transmutes to surrender by virtue of the intensity of our divine giving up. Indeed, that tension and intensity can propel us into a more expanded consciousness. Eventually, we may realize we do, in fact, have the opportunity to choose to learn and open through more gentle ways, but may we never shun the way we get there. Life is mysterious, and we come here to learn different things in different ways. Be gentle with yourself.

Giving It Back to God

As mentioned before, the intensity of suffering and pain can become so great that it turns into a wild, transmutative fire, and when it does, we bear witness to another pivotal moment in the ceremony of life. In these critical moments when our hearts break, when we realize there is *absolutely nothing we can do*, a great wave of divine surrender takes us. Giving up is often the last resort in these moments, and it comes because we cannot fight *for that which we thought we knew* any longer. The fight is over. Love wins even in the most seemingly destitute of moments.

This is the way of giving it back to God, of allowing that which is meant to move out of your system and back to the Divine, whether that be feelings of pain or anything else, to do so. Whatever is moving, whatever needs to be unstuck or released, can be simply given back to God. Yes, it is as simple and subtle as that. All energy is sacred; it is only the judging mind that has a hierarchy in which "positive" feelings are cherished and "negative" feelings are abhorred. As far as the universe is concerned, all energy is vital—regardless of its vibration—and we can always offer anything within us back to the light of God for transmutation. The creative core of anything contains within it the divine principle, which is always useful and unconditionally welcomed by God. Consider it: while you may only value the diamonds in your watch, to the watchmaker, even its most tiny scraps of metal are precious. Although we have forgotten so much, the divine energy of creation always instantly knows exactly what to do, even when we do not. This also means the divine energy of creation that lives within us always knows how to render our prayers and intentions, even if we do not understand or realize what is happening on that subtle level.

You are always welcome to simply offer back energy to God. You can do this through prayer, through meditation, through movement, through intention, or any other way you feel, and through simply knowing, "Yes, I am offering this back." Remember that we are all fine-tuning our senses and that in this *giving back*, we are tuning in to a very subtle language and communication. Never expect much from the subtlety; only your mind and ego can need a big show and presentation before they can be convinced. The heart of hearts is charmed by simplicity. And so, too, are you.

Face the Fury or Excavate the Gold?

As mentioned earlier, when we encounter pain, each of us must discern and honor the response that is best for us in our moment, whether that's simply being taken by the experience or doing the digging work to discover the teaching. Allow me to give you two examples of what I mean.

I will always remember the day that I truly believed I might be losing my mind. I was terrified, and I was suffering. I felt dangerously, nervously, and suddenly reckless inside, out of control, skating around the edge of sanity. It felt that way because I was going so close to the core of a very unhealthy paradigm of my mind. I cannot explain it in more detail than that, because it was very abstract and mysterious, but I knew that if I were to move through it, I had to do it then, as it was happening, and not once I had answers to questions or understood it more. I was being taken by a storm.

I was on the phone with an ex-boyfriend, sharing what I was experiencing. I had called him because I was afraid. I was hoping the solace of his voice and the safety and security of his presence would bring me back to the shore of sanity.

However, he was growing more and more concerned by the moment. There was a critical point in the conversation where he yelled at me, demanding I calm down, which, as you can imagine, only aggravated the situation inside me. He did not know what to do and was nervous, and his yelling was his attempt to help snap me back into "reality."

What his yelling did, though, was send me deeper into the intolerable confusion I was in the midst of. (We always get what we need!) I panicked, began to speak nonsensically, and then hung up the phone so I could be alone for this breakdown. I realized, "Fuck, whatever this is, wherever it is taking me, I have to face it, and if I go crazy, whatever, because I definitely cannot stave this off any longer. If I am crazy, at least I will be crazy in peace! This is where I am being taken. This is what is happening. This is me. I cannot fight this."

I let go. I gave in to the fury. I felt like I was traveling into insanity, and perhaps that is where I went. I cried as I burned, and although I was lost and unidentifiable within it, still I watched on. And then all of a sudden, the tears stopped. All of a sudden, there was simplicity and clarity and peace. And I never felt the same again. It was clear a dysfunction had been burned, had disappeared, and I was infinitely more at peace from that day on.

You see, I did not need to know what it was. I did not ask *why* or analyze it, and I knew to ask it to stop and to resist it would be detrimental. The only thing I could naturally do was give up and let go, and so I let that happen. I could not care; I had no attachment to the outcome: "This will take me to peace, or this will make me definitively crazy." It did not matter. The only thing that mattered was that the storm had arrived, and the only thing I could do was let it take me. It wasn't time to inquire. No, it was time to be thrust and thrown and blown apart.

It would have been much easier to have taken cover somewhere within myself by perhaps putting on a movie and distracting myself. But I knew I would be lying to myself if I did that, and for me, lying to myself is never an option. I would never put on a movie in the midst of an inner crisis. I knew you have to be willing to die if you want to live. You have to be willing to be completely destroyed if you are to find that which is indestructible within you. This is what it means to face your demons, to confront your fears, and to not stop short of freedom. To live life is to face it, and to not face it is to not know your true Self and to be unavailable and blind to the magic. Only in retrospect, years later, did I recognize that experience broke the paradigm of suffering that had hitherto been deeply rooted in my mind.

In this situation, surrender was what I needed. On another occasion in Guatemala a couple of years ago, digging to discover what I was trying to learn was the key to resolution.

While moving out of a house I had been living in, I walked downhill on a rocky alleyway and tripped and fell. It was quite a dive. My leg was hurt, but my knee took the brunt of the fall. I lay there for a few minutes before getting up, witnessing the act of having fallen and then lying there, humbly on the earth, having had no conscious ability to anticipate and therefore prevent the fall. I felt the throbbing pain and understood that going slow was needed. I breathed into it, and only when I was sure I was ready did I gently stand back up.

It was clear some damage had been done. My femur bone was turning inward, my knee was bleeding profusely, and I was in a lot of pain. It seemed to be the worst injury I'd experienced in my life.

I hobbled to the hostel I would be staying in for the next four days, got some ice, and laid down. I was very shaken up and concerned, since knee injuries can turn into quite the story. I knew there was damage, but not knowing what to do to help myself and feeling strongly that I should do nothing, I just lay down, watched an episode of *Modern Family*, and then hung out with my friend, Erin, who had come to visit. Erin and I had a conversation that helped me pinpoint how and why I had invited this injury to happen.

In this case, I was trying to learn how to relate with everyone and that I did not need to put myself in situations or with people I was not feeling compelled to be with (and, therefore, move myself out of alignment) as a way of learning that. How did I know it was true that this was what I was subconsciously attempting to learn? Simply because when it was uncovered in our discussion, *it resonated*, which is enough. This injury happened as I left a house I had been sharing with other people who I did not feel I should be sharing such intimate space with. Falling was a way of catching my attention so I would acknowledge this feeling, and it was also a small form of self-punishment for feeling guilty about feeling I should not be living with these people. They were wonderful, beautiful people; I just simply did not feel I should be there in the house with them.

The next day, I did my best to carry on despite the injury, but the pain and the state of things was undeniable. I attempted to go to a doctor, but alas, the office was closed, and there was not another one close by. That night, frustrated and feeling defeated, and with the pain increasing by the hour, I sensed the invitation to take matters more into my own hands. I worked with this challenging moment as an opportunity to remember the depth of my power, and I turned my attention inward for meditation. I held in my heart the teachings that wished to be welcomed in this moment, and through the voice of my intention said to God, "Take me to the miraculous healing—now." I channeled all of that pain and frustration I felt into the intention of a miracle.

During this meditation, I was shown that pain is just memory trapped in time. This was the guiding focus of the miraculous healing. I watched the pain that had been captured in my knee from the moment of falling release into the ether. I went to sleep directly after, and when I woke up, there was no trace of an injury. It was like nothing had ever happened.

I received invaluable insight from this situation. First, although the pain was physical, the frustration and the anger I felt were emotional. I was reminded that these feelings can be fuel for the fire of creation, if only we choose to direct them. Not only that, but whether the pain is physical or emotional, the way it is stored in the body is very similar. Second, I realized that pain is memory trapped in time, a powerful analogy that helped me understand how to work with its release. Finally, I was reminded of the power of prayer. All prayers are heard by God and are answered, even if we do not always understand, notice, or recognize the response.

Everything Is Made of Love

This discussion culminates like this: the core of everything that exists is love, for love is the creative principle that creates all. Many of the best "healers" in the world will tell you that when they work, they are simply channels of unconditional love and that this love is doing everything. The Divine is melting and transforming that which is stuck within a person back into its core pulse of love. The healer is not healing anything; he or she is just a channel for the Divine.

Now, we have not been taught how to transform the energy within us at all. And I mean *not at all*. Because for the most part, we live in a very cerebral and commercialized world, and quite simply, there's no money in us knowing how to heal on our own. We have been taught to numb pain with pills and psychoanalyze ourselves to death. So, fair enough, most of us are not yet fully tapped into the panacea of love melts all. But if you can tune in to the possibility that love is the core of everything, and if that truth resonates, then you can also tune in to the possibility that love is at the core of pain, heartbreak, and stagnation. And then you can begin to fathom the possibility that you can treat yourself with this sort of compassionate handling and bear witness to your own miraculous "healing."

As discussed, we tend to reject that which we do not recognize or know. That is the base reaction of the mind/ego to all that is unfamiliar. Why? Again, because until we know what something is, it is perceived as a threat, simply because of the possibility that it *might* kill us or *might* destroy our potential to be loved. (*Very primal*, I know, and are you noticing the trend here? Until we know better, we battle everything that our subconscious minds and egos perceive as a potential threat to our survival and ability to be loved, which are largely understood as essentially the same thing.)

Feelings we associate with darkness (like sadness and anger) are feared in their full extent because we don't know what else might be with them, like monsters, demons, bad memories, or black waves of darkness that might consume us—none of which is a true possibility. Our *belief* in them can consume us, but they themselves cannot, for they do not actually exist. If we can just tune in to this consideration, too, and begin to soak it in, then subconsciously this misaligned belief will begin to resolve itself. As we begin to accept and/or recognize everything as love, that the root of *everything* is love, we stop equating only light and joy with love, and our experience with the feelings passing through us changes. Then we are able to notice how contraction begins in moments we wish would go away, and we can choose to keep breathing and tune in to the frequency of the love within that contraction. The more and more we honor ourselves like this, the more we create as our Self truly intends to.

When you feel deep in the darkness, it can be very hard to know you are connected to the love core of all. But if you can trust that it is so, that trust will turn into a lighthouse.

Now, although yes, love does melt all into love, it cannot erase any pain you are still denying. Why? Because your denial becomes your command, and life can only reflect back to you what you are willing to see. The very presence of denial is the resistance of love. And if there is resistance, there is separation, and there is struggle because you are fighting your own inherent nature of being in oneness. Regardless of where you are, though, know that if you just let yourself go through a wild catharsis, old energy can transform into open space. Move into the perspective of love, and you will begin to recognize all as love. Love is that which accepts your hard spots, and through this acceptance, old wounds are liberated and released.

Part Three

MOVEMENT TOWARD TRUTH

Embodying Our Sacred Nature
of Creator and Created

Chapter 12
THE PATHLESS PATH

[Zen] does not confuse spirituality with thinking about God while one is peeling potatoes. Zen spirituality is just to peel the potatoes.

ALAN WATTS, *The Way of Zen*

When we allow life to simply be what it is, we see that it is, in fact, pathless. When now—*this moment*—is all there is, any "path" is a mere projection of and assumption about the future. A path that is rooted in the present moment can only be pathless. The pathless path is the one that is alive and dynamic, the one that is open to the resonance of truth revealing that which is spontaneous and unexpected. The pathless path is only a path in the sense that it is a way of living, and it is only truly our way when it becomes embodied.

Life evolves without a goal, for the magnetism of life is a creative force that continues on. This flow is embedded within us, and we are embedded within this flow. We are created from this impulse, and we carry on because of it. Although we are not in control of it, we can work great magic with it when we become aware of it.

If life goes on moving and shifting and responding to an infinite stream of new moments, then naturally, we do, too. When we are honoring that which is right for us, we are simply honoring that which is right for us *in this given moment*, for if we are to be honest, then we know the deepest truth is that anything and everything may change—and at a moment's notice, at that. If we are to be open to our lives harmonizing with our truths, then we must acknowledge how grand the scale of possibilities is and how life, in its ever-changing mystery, may surprise us. We must welcome the surprises of life if we are to truly experience the potential of being alive.

Only by honoring the greater truths (the macrocosmic truth) may we begin to honor our subjective truths (our microcosmic truth). This is recognition of the greater mystery of life and a deep honoring of being a child of that great mystery. In that profound recognition rests the awareness that the same macrocosmic mystery is within us, and it manifests and takes its course in many ways. When we simply recognize this fundamental aspect of the nature of existence, we can begin to understand its presence in our lives. And then finding ourselves moving away from the career or relationship we thought we'd be in for the rest of our lives is less of a shock or a "something must be wrong" and more of a deep, humble sigh of "alright, okay, here we go, and so it is." This is the way life moves. We do not hold the reins, and to feign so creates only pain. Evolution necessitates change.

When we deeply understand what it means that we are constantly evolving, we know how integral our life as the eternal student is to the whole. We know how imperative it is that we rise each morning open to what life gives us, humble to the subtle language of the Divine, which is so powerful and yet so soft. We begin to realize that to tune in to this language is to save our life, and that within the quiet coincidences of life rests great meaning. We realize that our only job is to trust the mysteriously divine flow, and that only through this humility may we move into the deepest alignment and be dazzled by the magic of life.

The abundant, benevolent nature of life, which comes alive upon what we are affectionately referring to as "the pathless path," demands no specific loyalty. In fact, to juice it in all its glory requires a presence so total that any path dissolves. Within Jesus, Buddha, John Lennon, and Rumi was the same beating heart. And it is the same beating heart that rests at the core of all of us. No matter where we go or how we get there, the door we all arrive at when we return home is exactly the same. And it's not that we arrive at the same version or copy of the door as one another. No, it's exactly the same *One*.

The pathless path grows within us all from the seed of humility. In our humility, we know that life knows best and will show us the way. This is the *yes* within that holds the subjective vision of our lives in good relation to the one great flow. It's the *yes* that says, "Hey, this may work for me today. This may be what I need today and what's flowing today, but I know that this may change. And if it does, indeed, change, that does not negate or invalidate this moment. It just means that it has changed for me. This moment takes me to all other moments. And so I say *yes* only to that which resonates as true to me in its moment. If I say no to your dinner invitation, it's because I'm saying *yes* to being alone tonight, which is what I need."

This fluid embodiment of the flow of what's right for us on a moment-to-moment basis is what deepens and inspires our aliveness and keeps us in harmony with the greatest possibilities for our lives. We are all shifting and discovering in every moment, and to align with that aspect of our nature is to align with the great visions and manifestations of the Self.

The Foundation of the Pathless Path

On a daily basis, we may have commitments that are right for us, and honoring them is in no way contrary to the pathless nature we speak of here. I want to point that out because most of us lead lives that are full of commitments, and commitments are very important if we are to ground out and create well in this life. The pathless path is not about following impulsiveness or abandoning long-term projects and relationships that, in challenging moments, we may intensely want to break out of and be tempted to trick ourselves into believing are no longer right for us. Because we see in others what we feel within ourselves, it is not uncommon for us to project our own need for more inner freedom onto our relationships, believing it to be a need for external freedom. If we depart from our beloveds based on that reflection, then we essentially are turning away from that reflection and, therefore, ourselves. Often, the pathless path includes *remaining*. When our loyalty is to our Selves and to the present moment, it is important to discern the spiritualized tricks of the ego that may tempt us into greener, more "free" pastures. Indeed, we may want to run away from relationships in their most challenging moments, yet if we work through those moments in a good way and stay present with our deepest truth, we will often find that our truth is to remain together.

Those challenging moments that require our trust, patience, and maximum showing-up-ness are very different from discovering something is truly no longer right for us. The pathless path is about deepening our listening to and honoring of the divine guidance of both life and our Selves. In doing so, we discover what is truly right for us and let it take us where it will. We can be sure that this way of life will miraculously, continuously take us to the most desirable and true visions of our Selves, manifest.

What inspires us today may change tomorrow. What is right for us in one moment may be the worst possible thing for us in another. Only when we stop identifying ourselves can we allow the river of life to take over. The mind will project the patterns of what did and did not work before, and subconscious beliefs will continue to surface to a potentially influencing degree. Nevertheless, it is our duty to our Selves and to the blossoming of our lives to not fall for what the mind is doing. May we see it and let it be there when it is, but never fall for it. And if we do find ourselves falling for it, may we catch ourselves and return to the innocence of the present moment and the heart.

You may do this a million times: trust your return to the present moment every time. Over and over again, just keep coming back.

EXPECTATIONS, ANTICIPATION, AND MANIFESTATION

"You see what you expect to see, Severus," said Dumbledore.

J. K. ROWLING, *Harry Potter and the Deathly Hallows*

We have all been warned about the pitfalls of having expectations, but when we look at them a bit more closely, we can actually extract some golden insights. To begin: to be in the state of expecting is to be connected to the future, which isn't necessarily a bad thing or the antithesis of being present. You can actually work great magic by connecting to the future. In fact, in order to manifest our visions and our intentions, we *must* connect with the future.

If life is one grand symphony, then we are maestros of the orchestras of our worlds. As the maestros, we direct the creation of the masterpieces that are played. Indeed, we have the ability to command the instruments to play and to tell them which chords and keys to play.

In this metaphor, when we are *conducting*, we are working with the ingredients of both the seen and the unseen worlds, all of which are the instruments. Through this process of manifestation, with the Divine, we can co-create and communicate into existence the life that feels right for us. We communicate it into existence by virtue of our intention, prayer, and focus, all of which are ways we silently communicate with the Divine.

While we do have the ability to communicate like this and command our visions into life by directing the orchestra, we do not have the ability to create the sound. While the directing is the show of our will, the sounds that come through the instruments are the play of mystery. These sounds that arrive per our commands and communication are comparable to the path through which our life and visions manifest. That sound is pure God stuff. It is the higher, omniscient will that comes through the instruments. It is the objective truth that aligns and purifies our subjective truth. The objective truth that aligns us with the "highest good," you could say.

So we can conduct the orchestra, but we cannot both conduct the orchestra *and* play the instruments at the same time. The orchestra will share through its sounds the vibration of that which we are calling into existence, and those vibrations will form it into life. And those sounds, that *divine will*, happens entirely on its own, mused through your totality, your awareness, and your focused intention on conducting as the grand master of your life.

The orchestra plays a series of musical pieces. Each one of these pieces has sheet music. Now focus on this: *you* have within you the sheet music for your life. Time is irrelevant in the space of this vision because time is an aspect of three-dimensional life. The place from which you are conducting, however, is absolutely timeless.

Your sheet music is created by God. You receive it by opening up to knowing and accepting the next step or the vision of what is best for you in this moment in life. You *channel* it. You get the vision, you get the feeling *associated* with the vision, and that becomes your sheet music. So it's a four-step meditation process: you open up and request this vision, you receive the sheet music, you communicate your *yes* by conducting it into existence, and then the music/manifestation unfolds according to God's will.

Intensely focused on your sheet music, you stand before the orchestra of the seen and unseen, and you conduct through the unfathomable power of your intention. You say, "Go!" and you call in the fire. You call in the burning of the old beliefs that could have stood in your way. You call in the highest light to carry forth your vision. You release that which limits you. You focus intensely on the unfolding of this piece of music, and naturally, nothing enters this music that is not a part of it. It is a moment of deep, intimate union between you and God, and the vibration is so high that the only things that can maintain existence there are your awareness and the symphony itself. In this moment, you are in divine dialogue.

When we talk about the sheet music and the orchestra playing the song, notice the relevance of the future. Notice how its feeling is entirely different from the time-space one we get when we reference the future in normal daily life. This is something else. When you go to conduct the orchestra, the beginning and the end of the song are already known. There is a future aspect, but it's a future aspect that has to do with the energy of life, which never begins and never ends. This is you tapping into that depth, that timelessness of your visions. So as we manifest and co-create with the Divine through our Selves, an aspect of "future" is needed, but it is the aspect of timelessness. You can think of it as enlightened time, if you like.

Now, here is where expectations come in and how the whole thing gets confused. We are hardwired to know how to conduct the orchestra. In less conscious ways, we have been doing it our entire lives, all the time. But our internal impulses that come from divine seeds have been manipulated by the mind to seem like superficial patterns (like expectations). When it comes to knowing how to manifest and how to work with the timeless nature of existence, we see the trip-up happen around the matter of time.

Timelessness is an aspect of our being. Deep within, we know that we need a connection to the future if we are to create in this dimension. However, when that timelessness is interpreted through less sentient gateways, such as the ego/mind, it's concluded that we only exist if we also exist in the future (and the past). In other words, the ego/mind identifies with time, and our identity/existence becomes defined by who we were in the past and what we will be in the future. And, as we know, when we are identified with something, we believe we *are* that, and then we try to control for safety and love.

The healthy, illuminated version of this connection to the future looks like what we have just unveiled: the maestro and the orchestra. The grand master of life. In the unhealthy/isolated version, the mind processes this tick of "connection to future" as a need to control, which often turns into a need to feel secure that we will go on existing in a way we believe to be safe. So the immortal voice of manifestation rises up through our knowingness and gets distorted as it goes through the mind channel, primarily because the human consciousness has been asleep for such a long time and already has many patterns in place. The mind channel distorts it into urgency, into control, in its attempt to form patterns based on belief and past experiences. This, then, is projected into the future. This is what makes us feel safe.

Indeed, the mind gets stimulated by the primordial internal impulse of creation and manifestation, and it becomes uncomfortable. It does not understand timelessness and the raw tick of *anticipation*, so it scrambles to make sense of what it is receiving. In that process, reactions get triggered through the body, emotions, and the mind. In an attempt to calm itself, the mind creates the phenomena of *expectations* to feel safe, to feel like it understands something about its world.

This process has gone on for so long without being noticed that it has become totally normal to have expectations. Expectations have become a part of daily life and are regarded as either something totally fine and normal or something to moderate and keep in check. But we have the opportunity to extract a golden nugget of wisdom from the experience of having expectations and, from it, learn how to better manifest in our lives. Furthermore, as we get to the root of expectations, including what they are and where they come from, if it resonates, we can acknowledge this as what is happening within ourselves and, by virtue of the illumination, allow the energetic cords to untangle.

When there are expectations, there is an anticipation of what is to come. This anticipation comes from the divine impulse of creation. It's the smile that comes the moment before the beloved leans in for a kiss. In the space of timelessness and willing and receiving the life of our visions, we know of their inevitability just like we know the end of the musical piece, and therefore there is a very pure and gentle anticipation. It is the kiss that begets the kiss. The kiss itself includes the next kiss. It is the waving of the hand that calls in the next melody. The way the maestro's hand moves through air includes the movement into the next moment, the anticipation.

The energy of anticipation can be likened to a fishing line that allows the Divine to pull in the bounty in its own time. There is the motion of pulling toward. In its purity, this motion is divine and part of the grand alchemy. However, processed by the mind, this motion can become distorted and turn into wanting, impatience, and yearning. The gap of waiting is very third dimensional.

So we are talking about cleansing two aspects related to expectations. One is the anticipation, so that it may rest again as the energetic counterpart to that which is manifesting—the fishing line moved only by God, never the impulses of the mind. Moved only by love, never fear. Trusting all aspects of the arrival of what's being manifested.

The other aspect to cleanse is the need for control. Here is an example of how this aspect plays out. Isaac is sitting at his office desk on a Friday, 4:45 p.m. He's watching the clock tick by. He is going on his third date with Jessie at 9 p.m. Finished with his work obligations and just waiting for the day to end, he puts on Pink Floyd and is instantly brought into his heart: a melty, swirly place where love begins to flow. He gets a vision of Jessie, which leads to a vision of him kissing her, and he becomes excited. The impulse, the raw material of anticipation (again, that raw manifestation material of the universe), rises to his mind, where it is captured for inspection and control: *What is this vision? Will I kiss Jessie? Do I even want to kiss Jessie? The last girl I kissed on the second date never returned my calls. My mother always told me how much she appreciated my father waiting until their third date for a kiss. If I kiss Jessie tonight, she may never want to see me again.*

These beliefs and these thoughts of the past and future, brought up by his mind, followed Isaac along as he met Jessie, then lurked in the background as they went on their date. They were so distracting that he missed the energy of anticipation that was building—energy that would have told him Jessie was actually dying for a kiss and inspired his body to lean in and give it. His expectations held him back, and in the end, Jessie was turned off by Isaac's lack of presence and holding back. Expectations killed anticipation and the life of the kiss-to-be.

The mind employs expectation to minimize risk and make sense of life. If life is predictable, it is more safe. If we can predict life, we can minimize the possibility of pain and devastation. Do you see how robotic this is? Life is meant to be wild, crazy, free. We all know how painful and dull slipping into the robotic state is. Western societies, by design, encourage our roboticness, so we need to be careful and really make a decision to break out of it for it to happen. The robotic way is not the way of the heart and the Self; rather, it is a path that leads to painful sterilization, to the solidifying of the heart into muted steel.

Every time an expectation arises, you have the invitation to gently examine it. I don't mean analyze it; I mean gently examine it with awareness. To be sure, not every single expectation we have is a big deal, but understanding the nature of how expectations exist at all, as mentioned before, is empowering, liberating, and, depending on what we do with the wisdom, resolving. When the more benign variety of expectations arises, like, "I expect my mother to call me back tonight," we can just notice it. When the stories around our expectations gain decoration and may potentially influence our state of being or our behavior, such as, "I expect the person I'm dating to call me on the phone to get to know me" (and if he doesn't, I will panic), we begin to have the opportunity to catch ourselves and anchor ourselves into greater presence and less certainty about the way things "should" happen. The energy around our expectations can vary from one expectation to the other, but even in their most intense form, they're just more of those flags that say, "Dig here." What are we trying to control? Where are we still afraid? What propels us out of presence? Where can we melt into surrender, into trust, and let life be more unpredictable?

When we are in expectation, we are not open to what life is going to show us. Instead, we already have an idea of how it should look or will look, and so that is what we project into manifestation. When this is happening, our magic wands are being greatly misused. Like a child holding a gun who has no idea of the consequential power in his hands, when we are influenced by expectations, we, too, may create that which we do not truly desire to create and, in doing so, diminish the potential of our own lives.

Life is full of surprises, many of which are grand and fulfilling beyond our wildest imagination. Just consider how little access we have even to our own brains. We know so very little about the spectrum of energy and universal life. Life is capable of delivering the most incredible moments and gifts to us, if only we allow it to. When we are in a state of expectation, we are placing ceilings over the potential of what we can experience. Blow off the roof and let life show you what it's got. That's the only way it can.

When we're communicating with life from the space of expectation, we are communicating unconsciously from the space of duality. And so we will get more of that. We will get more dualistic feelings and experiences until we move into a space of meditation with life, where we are rooted in union and watching the duality play out from there. Then we will be actively engaging with life in the co-creation of our most divine experience, having given up our ideas of what should be, and instead allowing what is meant to be—that which will be the most meaningful, most fulfilling, and the most heart exploding—to truly pour through us. You receive the musical sheet of vision, you say, "Yes, let's play," and the music unfolds as it will.

And we must remember to watch ourselves: it can be easy to have expectations about how our visions will play out. Life is so profoundly mysterious. Often our visions and what is right for us in one moment will not end or play out the way we imagine they would. Often our visions lead us to a new vision, which leads us to a new vision, of which each vision and each step is divine and creates the whole of our life. Only in our simplicity can we grasp and welcome this.

May we remember, that which is known—that which is *true*—needs no expectation. You do not expect your beloved to love you; you simply know it is so. You do not expect the sun to rise; it simply is so that the sun will rise. That which is, is. Expectation is present only where divine knowing has not yet set in. And as we settle more into the home within our Selves, to simply be present and open, alive and thriving, is realized as *enough*.

Chapter 14

FROM WANTING
TO DESIRE

And as is his desire, so is his will; and as is his will, so is his deed;
and whatever deed he does, that he will reap.

MAHENDRA KULSHRESTHA, *The Golden Book of Upanishads*
(F. Max Muller, translator)

It is often said that desire is the root of suffering, and many of us believe it. But the root of suffering could never be desire itself. Instead, it is desiring something to be any other way than the way it is, which, by virtue of its context and texture, is a *want*. Why? Because the mind came up with it. The mind, in its resistance to life as it is, *wants* things to be different, whereas desire exists in the heart and soul as the spirit of inspiration itself. It has been said, after all, that it was Buddha's *desire* to relieve people of suffering that led him to uncover and share the great wisdom he knew. Wanting, you can do without, but desire is an invaluable part of the fabric of your being. Consider it like this: wanting is tense, desire is relaxed—passionate, but relaxed. The distinction between the two is important to be aware of, for to try to extinguish or deny the fire and desire of your heart is to mute and disempower the creative force within.

Let's zoom in to be touched by a deeper understanding. The first insight to tune in to is, *receiving cannot happen in the vessel of wanting*. Everything has a vibration. When you embody the energy of wanting, the vehicle of your being takes a particular shape—the shape of wanting. And in the shape of wanting, nothing can be truly received. Love cannot fit into this shape, prosperity cannot fit into this shape, peace cannot fit into this shape.

To truly receive, you must be formless. You must be open to the energy you are calling in and then be able to receive and hold it. To be one with it. Only when you are one with something are you truly receiving it; only then are you truly intimate with it, and only then can you truly know it, truly feel it. Only then can you dance with this energy, be moved by this energy, and only then can the chemistry of you plus this energy be revealed.

If you are wanting another person, there is no space for the other to meet you. There is only a tense vehicle of anxiety through which the stream of truth and fulfillment cannot flow. If you are wanting to feel differently than you are feeling, there is no acceptance. And when there is no acceptance, there is only resistance and, therefore, no possibility of transformation. There is no intimacy with the moment, no journey to unwrap the gifts.

And who can truly want? If there is nobody there—no person inside the person—who is wanting? Your pure essence can only accept, and the essence of your soul can only be inspired. The fountain of this inspiration overflows into the purity of desire.

Pure desire is divine fuel that attracts that which you are desiring. It's the *yes* in response to your anticipation of what's to come, what's right for you. Its song floats toward its resonance like gorgeous dancing smoke, luring its focus into manifestation. When your mind is too involved and attached, it is in wanting, which is very different. When the energy is the pure passion of your soul, detached and in surrender to what will be, guided by God, it is desire. Desire lights; desire is a microphone to God. It is the primary feeling that triggers manifestation, and its presence is a mandatory ingredient in alchemy.

Do you want your life to conform to the fictions of your mind, or does moving into divine openness feel more fulfilling, more true?

Here is a meditation for you: Relax as you watch the burnt branches of wanting snap in their futility. Breathe deeply as the old season cycles out. Enjoy the precious feeling of opening as space clears for the warm, golden rush of desire to carry your visions to realization. Every moment is an invitation home.

Chapter 15

THE POWER
OF LANGUAGE

Language is not the territory, but is the means by which change can be expressed. You can talk about change forever and become obsessed with the ideas and thoughts themselves. But in order for something really new to enter the world, language has to be used in a playful manner, as a means of expressing a frequency. It is the frequency that holds the energy of change. Language is simply the means of resonating the music.

RICHARD RUDD, *Gene Keys*

Words are magic. I repeat: Words. Are. Magic. I bet no onlooker observing the human race would ever guess that when paying attention to the way in which people use words. Words do, however, have a life of their own, and when we project them through ourselves and into the world through speaking, writing, and the thoughts we get involved with, we affirm *that which we are focusing upon.* That is our agreement. And from there, we muse their destiny into life.

Words live between worlds. Just as anyone can pretend smoking cigarettes is not harmful, we can choose to be ignorant about our language choices. In both cases, the fact remains the same: there are consequences. Words carry meaning, and when we project meaning into the world through the channels that we are, we call back and perpetuate that meaning, that energy. That which we put out comes back to us. The echoes of these words resound and permeate the womb of manifestation. So you can either carelessly *use* words or respectfully, intelligently *work with* them. Which is to say, you can either wave your wand with intelligence or with carelessness.

So how does it work? Well, words are symbols. They cast out the vibration of their meaning wherever they are, whether they are uttered, written, or thought. They are neither deadened nor encapsulated things. They do not have a protective shell around them. They are vibrant, evocative, and alive, and they're made more so by whatever intention and emotion you express them with. And like a paint color infused with hues, whatever energy you load up your words with determines their overall meaning, their volume, their tinge, and their trajectory. Words serve a gigantic purpose. They are one of the most powerful tools you have to shape your life and the world around you.

Either you can work *with* words, or in your ignorance, the words will work you. Either you cast spells with them, or you will fall under their spell. One of you is going to be running the show, so either you are directing or in your absence the words will, simply because it is the only thing they can do.

Just imagine this for a moment: You wake up in the morning and there is no hot water for your shower, you're out of coffee, your partner is stressing out. And then you receive an e-mail that tells you an important meeting you haven't yet prepared for has been moved from tomorrow to today. Understandably, you might experience annoyance or frustration in this situation. You might groan and say something like, "This is going to be a bad day. I can tell already." And if you do say or believe that thought, sure enough, by 9 p.m., you could probably look back and confirm that it was, indeed, a bad day.

Now, let's pause and consider this basic consideration of quantum mechanics: *nothing happens unless it is witnessed.* If a tree falls in the woods and no one hears it, did it fall? *You are the most important witness in your life.* When you say or think something, you witness yourself either saying or thinking it simply by being aware that you have said or thought this or that. To take it a step further, when you simply choose to believe what you think without speaking it, or you believe these thoughts and then channel them into reality by speaking them, you confirm it as reality and create a trajectory. By virtue of your attaching to a thought and getting onto its bandwagon, you set forth its actualization. Your witnessing and then your acceptance of it is your "agreement," and that is what linguistically propels things into existence, into actually happening.

This aspect of creating your reality is a very subtle art. It is not about resisting what is happening or denying anything at all. Rather, it is about redirecting the focus of your awareness, your *witnessing*, away from the fictions of the mind and intently upon that which you desire most for your true life, for the life that stirs your soul into vivid aliveness and leaves a trail of flower blossoms in your wake.

So let's apply the wisdom to the above example. Moment/ opportunity one is the arrival of the thought: "The morning has been challenging, therefore, today is going to be a bad day." This thought is just another houseguest of sorts, like floating debris that enters through the back door. In the present moment, all is well. You have full power of choice to interact/respond like this, communicated via your nonreaction: "Yeah, okay, you can pass through, and I will watch as you go on your way." On the other hand, if you react (rather than respond) and get onboard—if you start shrieking, "Ah! There is garbage blowing in, and it's all over the floor! Quick, close the doors, shut the windows!"—you are then agreeing with it and closing it in. Then you're saying,

"Yeah, this is my story right now, the garbage-on-the-floor story. Let's fall for it again." And that, I have come to know, is how it works. This metaphysical formula is hugely powerful, and your awareness of it perhaps even more so. Your agreement with the belief or thought, your energizing of the story, is what powers it into life. Without that, it's a lifeless possibility.

It's not a big deal (that is to say, it does not equate to damaging your life) to think or say something not completely supportive or ideal. We are all human, and it is normal to experience the spectrum of duality, to notice the pendulum swinging perhaps a bit more than we might like and to unintentionally move with it. Likewise, it's important to not take all of this too seriously. Life is a journey of continuously coming back to your center and the present moment. The key is in how you clean it up and what you do with it. The key is in how you narrate your life and the energy you embody. The key is in waking up to the magic that is everywhere.

When you do not get involved with the limiting thoughts and beliefs that pass through you, they become limp and power-less. Your focus is the only thing capable of enlivening them. In other words, you are the God of the thoughts that pass through your inner sky in the form of words. The ones you focus upon come alive by virtue of your attention to them. The ones you simply notice and let pass remain nothing more than an empty possibility, unchosen. So, all thoughts begin as monochromatic, empty shells. You focus on them and thereby confirm your agreement; they gain color, life, vibration. You let them pass without selection, and they remain a benign effigy until they totally fade out of the sky. Going, going, gone. Indeed, one of the best things we can know is what to ignore.

Language—verbal, nonverbal, thoughts—is a canon of possibilities. Language is filled with symbols. Every smile is a symbol. Every kiss is a symbol. Every "fuck you," every "today is gorgeous," every "it's all good"—they are all symbols. You, and you alone, choose which ones paint your life.

Say you're at a restaurant having dinner with your friend on a day that's been pretty hard. She asks how you're doing, and you tell her, "I never heard back from that company I pitched my project to. It's so hard to make money in this town." Now, you had a hard day, and I'm not saying to not honor that. But I am saying to pick words that reflect what you *really* mean. Not only do you then express yourself more accurately and create an empowered and clear, truthful conversation, but you also support the good manifestations in your life. Consider this more truthful wording in response to your now worried friend: "It's been two weeks since I wrote that company I pitched, and I'm eager to hear back. Not to mention I would really benefit from this job coming through." The rest of your dialogue, whether to your friend or to yourself via a sentient assimilation and perspective shift, would go, "I am just going to relax and put good energy on it and perhaps check in with them tomorrow, if that feels right. If it's best for me for it to happen, then it will. Otherwise, I trust something else will pop up that I will enjoy even more." And *ta-da!* You have turned into a good magician!

To help us all out a bit more, here is a list of common things we say and often believe, and truthful, supportive turnarounds. The expressions listed below are considered "limiting magic" specifically when they are *believed*, versus when we embody the understanding that the expression is not truth and is something we may shift. For example, if I say, "I'm sick" and I believe I am this sickness to the extent that I accept it as truth and project it into the future, then I'm in limiting magic. However, if I am simply expressing that I'm sick *right now*, and I embody the supportive core listed below, then the trajectory is supportive of me. Ultimately, the energy behind our words is everything.

The turnarounds include potential inner dialogue (for sentient consideration) and perspective shifts. Notice how we are not giving them a glaze of pretty words or rote affirmations; rather, we are aligning them with the simple, storyless, open-ended truth of the present moment. In this way, we give the Divine space to work good magic with us rather than squeezing it out with limiting agreements and interpretations. The truthful, supportive cores of each thought function as the energy behind the words and are not offered in the spirit of optimism; rather, they are possible reflections of an aligned perspective that works for your highest good, and they are invitations to sense and embody that perspective (or whatever perspective is true for you). Remember, there is gold within every situation, and when your language is consistent with that, you get closer to discovering it.

LIMITING MAGIC	*I'm sick. I'm depressed.*
TRAJECTORY	Identified with sickness/depression. Projecting it into the future and prolonging it.
TRUTHFUL & SUPPORTIVE CORE	*I'm not feeling well at the moment, and I'm listening to my inner voice to discover what I need to feel healthy again. I'm passing through a hard moment, and it's okay. I'm working with it. It has been challenging lately, and all is well throughout it all.*
POSSIBLE TEACHING	Slow down. Rest. Take some time off. Research corresponding ailment/organ and its metaphysical connection (e.g., liver and anger, heart and emotions/love,

lungs and sadness/grief). Not labeling or judging yourself; self-acceptance. Moving beyond attachments. Discovering what is between you and "happiness." Silence. Resolving past wounds. Releasing expectations about how you *should* feel.

ᵛ ᵃ ᵛ

LIMITING MAGIC	*Quitting smoking is impossible. I can't do it!*
TRAJECTORY	Perpetuates a cycle of behavior. Gives away power.
TRUTHFUL & SUPPORTIVE CORE	*I love smoking, and it is challenging to quit. But I have decided to. It feels impossible, but I know it is completely possible—and I am choosing to do it now.*
POSSIBLE TEACHING	Look at the language, and you will discover that you're giving away your power. Nothing has control over you. You made the decision to begin smoking, and you can make the decision to stop. Changing habits is not supposed to be easy. Everything is a choice.

ᵛ ᵃ ᵛ

LIMITING MAGIC	*I'm such an idiot!* (Said in jest in response to something you did not understand.)

TRAJECTORY	Perpetuates subtle behavior of putting yourself down.
TRUTHFUL & SUPPORTIVE CORE	*Oh, I get it now! I missed that! Ha!*
POSSIBLE TEACHING	See how and when you shame yourself. There's nothing to be ashamed of. Are you afraid of shining your light? Do you feel unworthy of being beautiful and powerful? How does insecurity serve you?

❧ ☙ ❧

LIMITING MAGIC	*I'm sorry.* Specifically, the ritual of apology or the overuse of apologizing, often related to minuscule and benign things: *I can't get together tonight, sorry! Sorry for that typo. Oh, I have to call you back, sorry! Can we change the appointment? Sorry.* Also including the one-dimensional response of *I'm sorry* when resolution is what's needed.
TRAJECTORY	Disempowers you. Avoiding deeper resolution.
TRUTHFUL & SUPPORTIVE CORE	Eliminating all unnecessary use of the word *sorry* and ritual apology. Conveying simply what's true for you: *Actually, I'm not available on Friday. How about Wednesday?* Going deeper to resolve that which needs our attention.

POSSIBLE TEACHING	Do you deserve to do what you want? Do you know how to set boundaries? Do you know how to express your *no* in a supportive, truthful way? Did you grow up in a household where your desires were denied, or were you constantly told to apologize for just being yourself? You're allowed to be in your power. You can be accountable for yourself and own your decisions. You do not need to apologize for your life or for who you are.

❧ ⚜ ❧

LIMITING MAGIC	*I can't stand him/her.*
TRAJECTORY	Perpetuates a cycle of deflection and a lack of accountability for your feelings and yourself.
TRUTHFUL & SUPPORTIVE CORE	*It's time for me to choose to be around people I feel I want to be with. I find myself very triggered by her. I have a hard time with what her values seem to be. Hmmm, what does that teach me about myself?*
POSSIBLE TEACHING	Do I blame other people for how I feel? Can I see that I am responsible for my feelings? Learn what it means that others are your mirror. Why do you choose to spend time with people you do not enjoy? Do you feel unworthy of the

people you admire? How does judging others serve you?

❧ ❧ ❧

LIMITING MAGIC	*You* always *do this! I can't stand it!*
TRAJECTORY	This is accusatory and reactive. It creates an environment for a fight by putting the other on the defensive. It moves toward separation rather than unification in challenging relationship moments. It also adds confusion by using the word *always*, which is a judgment and is rarely true.
TRUTHFUL & SUPPORTIVE CORE	Take a deep breath and take time to cool off. *This [factual observation] happens a lot. It's really hard for me when it does. I would so appreciate a different version of this. I need X, Y, and Z. I would love to just work it out so we can enjoy more. Shall we work on it?* (Smile.) (Wink.) (Kiss.)
POSSIBLE TEACHING	Movement toward unification even in challenging moments. How can I create a supportive dialogue that honors both mine and my partner's needs? Nonviolent communication. It's better to be happy than "right." Honoring your need to take space to get clear before communicating.

❧ ❧ ❧

LIMITING MAGIC	*I hate this shirt. I look awful in this.*
TRAJECTORY	Creates a disempowered narrative.
TRUTHFUL & SUPPORTIVE CORE	Wear a different shirt and be nice to yourself.
POSSIBLE TEACHING	You deserve to feel great in what you're wearing. Why are you choosing to wear something you don't feel good in? Donate clothes you do not like or wear. Work toward feeling better in your body.

❧ ☙ ❧

LIMITING MAGIC	*I'm broke. I have no money right now* (expressed as a problem).
TRAJECTORY	Keeps you stuck in the problem paradigm. Attracts the so-called problem and not that which you desire to attract.
TRUTHFUL & SUPPORTIVE CORE	*It's a good thing I have the option to explore different work opportunities because I could really benefit from the cash. Do you know of any work opportunities? I am doing my best, putting my energy out there and working to make this happen, and I know life is in the process of bringing me something lucrative and great.*

Do you associate money with being evil or corrupt? Do you believe money and spirituality do not belong together? Do you deserve to be honored and get paid for your work? Does your work bring you joy? Focus on the outcome and how you and the Divine can work together to bring it to you. Focus on moving forward and on what you are creating.

❦ ❦ ❦

With the words and thoughts we empower, we cast magic spells all over our crazy little lives; over our homes and our spaces and our relationships. Every string of words is, in fact, a spell. There is only a small difference between the elusive magic spells that seem arcane and part of witchcraft and the spells of the words we use on a daily basis. The difference is *belief, intention*, and *awareness*. Spells, prayers, or any rituals that include highly charged words are backed by belief, intention, and awareness of the power of the words, which in turn increase their volume and charge. Without that awareness, the power may lessen, *but it's never eradicated*, which means all day long people are throwing around words that affect their lives and experiences without even realizing it. Magic not recognized as such is still magic; it's just the magic of a blind magician, and having all been blind magicians at some point in our lives, we can all imagine a few scenarios showing how that can turn out.

And when there is no awareness of the magic—of the prayer—then there is no gratitude, for if you are not aware of the incredible gifts you are working with, how can you be grateful for them? True gratitude—meaning gratitude that is known through feeling and not intellect—is a very powerful, high vibration, a potent and graceful energy that is present in every strong prayer. In a way, the energy of gratitude establishes connection with the Divine, because when we are in gratitude, we are in tangible, and therefore more easily witnessed, divine energy. God becomes so obviously present when we are basking in the grace of gratitude, because gratitude is an experience with the Divine. It's realizing, "The beauty of this is so beyond me and anything I could ever comprehend, all I can do is bow before the sky and say thank you." To tell you the truth, what I know to be true is that "thank you" is the only prayer there really is.

We've all got this magic. More accurately, we don't *have* it at all—we simply *are* it. We are divine awareness conducting magic and birthing miracles all over the place. Sometimes we just need to remember and dust off our magic wands.

Part Four

A CEREMONY CALLED LIFE

Remembering Life as the Spiritual Practice

Chapter 16

THE DOORWAY
TO MEANING

The first peace, which is the most important, is that which comes
within the souls of men when they realize their relationship, their
oneness, with the universe and all its Powers, and when they realize
that at the center of the universe dwells *Wankan-Tanka* [Great
Spirit], and that this center is really everywhere, it is within each of
us. This is the real Peace, and the others are but reflections of this.

NICHOLAS BLACK ELK,
The Sacred Pipe (recorded and edited by Joseph Epes Brown)

What we begin to realize is that life has been offered to us as a
ceremony for our awakening, for our enjoyment, and for the
expression of our creative potential—all of which are based in
meaning. Every day is a rite of passage, gifting us endless opportunities to know ourselves better, see more clearly, and create
the good visions of our lives. Through our willingness to discover the great meaning within the moments and experiences
that pass, we can unearth our sentient remembrance of the great
gift of life.

Indeed, we must pass through the doorway to meaning if
we are to arrive at the ceremony of life, which is revealed just
through the passageway. We must begin to surrender our gaze

to the Divine Perspective so we may, once more, hear, receive, and give in to the overflowing messages, enjoyment, peace, and invitations for growth that are embedded in all moments. When we are living this honestly, the wild ritual of life is at its best.

We do, in fact, have the supreme privilege of bringing our divine visions to life, defined as the sense of what our life looks and feels like when we are creating and expressing from the core of our truths. These visions could only ever be in harmony with God. The life of divine vision is always supported in manifesting because God came up with it—the Divine inspired it through our hearts in the first place. We are just channels for these visions. These are the visions that somehow, mysteriously, *are already so*, and so they are gently anticipated. These are the visions that we did not think up, that we do not want, but rather we *desire* because they are the integral, natural consequence of our existence, as felt in the core of our being. In a way, it is a remembering of ourselves and what our lives are to feel like, and we recall it from the timeless essence of *it having already happened* and bring it into the now. This is how we are turned on and how we light up, and, in turn, how we light up the world: simply by existing in our most natural expression, simply by being our true Self.

This sort of blossoming is predicated on the awareness of the great meaning of all things that happen and pass through our lives. This is not to suggest that every small conversation we have with every clerk at check-out must provide us with a great revelation; rather, it means that through each challenge and each simple moment we have the opportunity to drop more into presence, appreciation, and love, and when relevant, discover something to reflect upon for our growth.

These dysfunctions that we resolve are the sorts of obstructions that had hitherto prevented the carrying out of what we always knew to be true, to be fated—those small but deep visions we are full of conviction about and watch patiently, in trust, to be realized and to evolve. Indeed, as we free up the areas of dysfunction within us, we stop subconsciously cutting off our pure expression and the manifestation of our visions. Where these visions were once shut down, upon crossing an inner boundary they become clear to flow through us and bloom.

As we tune in to the great profundity of existence and its relevance to our microcosmic life, we choose to acclimate ourselves to its climate of meaningfulness. With one foot in front of the other and a flickering light, we walk steadfastly toward the only allegiance we ever truly had: the chapel of our soul. On our way there, the bell of truth rings and resounds through the entirety of our being, and we find ourselves pulled toward its undeniable sound, which trails like the scent of a warm pie beckoning a hungry wolf. Indeed, as truth and meaning bake within our hearts, the core appetite of our being is awakened to be served. This was all we ever wanted and all we ever needed: to remember life as profoundly meaningful. To remember life as the deliciously wild, sacred ceremony it is.

Simply because we have chosen to arrive at the ceremony and see the deep beauty and meaning of all things, we are supported and cleansed by the Divine. Our eyes are wiped with the sacred cloth for us to see the deep, inherent offerings of each moment and each happening of life—to see the presence of God and love in all. We have come back, and we are reoriented to go home.

And here we are now, upon that very fertile ground. This is the soil that nurtures the roots of our lives. This is the ground that embraces our joy, laughing in unison with us, opening up more space for our visions to come to life. This is the climate in which the Self's well-being thrives. This is the inner Garden of Eden, resurrected and restored.

Throughout it all, we notice how easy it is to slam to the ground on the other end of the seesaw, dust clouding our eyes. We see over and over again that we do, indeed, get thrown off, and that for as long as we are in this human form, we are in a precarious position that requires our compassion and attention. In light of this state of affairs, we choose to remember, even with hazy, stinging eyes, that we are *always* in the ceremony—could only ever *be* in ceremony—and in doing so, we walk again through the doorway of meaning for our eyes to be wiped once more. And this insistence will save our lives.

As we stand before this sacred doorway, we realize its response to us is conditional, albeit only in the sense that it's reflective. If we stand before it arrogant and haughty, indeed the door will remained locked. If we stand before it in doubt, it will disappear. If we knock upon it distracted, our minds somewhere else, we fail to see it open. Anyone in the world can go through it, and there could never be a key. Yet it opens only when we approach it in a certain, truthful way. Otherwise, we may not notice its openness and its infinite offering again and again.

To pass into this fertile land of meaning, we must arrive in reverence. We must approach the door in silence, focused upon the primordial pulse of our being and all of life. We must allow ourselves to open into acceptance, for within acceptance lives our accountability and, therefore, our ability to extract meaning for our growth—and the possibility for things to come to life. We must allow ourselves to be released into the current, the movement of acceptance, otherwise known as surrender, so that we may be taken and discovered unto ourselves. And once we are through, by God, we must celebrate, for what else is there to do?

In silence, we can hear. In acceptance, we receive the message and become impregnated by meaning. In surrender, we are taken into journey. And throughout, celebration is the dance, the miraculous movement of it all. Each of these four things—silence, acceptance, surrender, and celebration—is just an aspect of ourselves and our inherent divine nature, so let's take a closer look at them now, so that we may recognize their flavor and drop into their gifts more simply.

Chapter 17

DEEPENING INTO SILENCE

For

God

To make love,

For the divine alchemy to work,

The Pitcher needs a still cup.

Why

Ask Hafiz to say

Anything more about

Your most

Vital

Requirement?

HAFIZ, *The Gift: Poems by Hafiz* (Daniel Ladinsky, translator)

It is from the space of silence that we perceive the subtle language of life. Alert and listening from the quiet core of our beings, we become able to extract gold—the great meaning, teaching, and opportunity within not just the obvious moments of significance, but also the mundane ones, the impossibly challenging ones, and the ones that feel so destitute and cruel we're certain there is nothing for us but pain.

We have to keep bringing ourselves back to the silence if we are to become anchored within it. In a way, we could say that we must make a practice out of it, although really it is nothing more than an untraining of our energy so that we may stabilize in our true orientation within our Selves. With our anchoring in our inner silence comes our comfort, including our comfort in the mystery and the unknowingness of life, and letting it all unfold as it may. Indeed, the silence carries us deeper into the mystery, which is a treasure chest of ancient wisdom that guides us along the way. Because *we are silence*, our anchoring in this silence is the very orientation that keeps us aligned with both truth itself and *our* truths, and so we must drop more and more into this inner space through all moments of life. To be sure, that requires our commitment, dedication, and focus, and, at least in the beginning, if not ongoingly, a daily practice of meditation. It is through our growing comfort and meeting with our essential inner nature of silence that our anchoring can really have a chance to drop.

Often, prior to our cultivation of a meditation practice, when fear arises in response to the meeting with our nature of nothingness, an impulse to create stories arrives as the ego attempts to make sense of it all and fill the nothingness with "meaning" in the form of details. In other words, to the ego, *something* is always better than *nothing*. As we get comfortable in the unknowingness of life and the nothingness within, and as we come to know and accept our true nature, the impulse to narrate ourselves out of the silence will fade.

We must drop into this silence because it is our essence and the fabric of existence, and for that, it holds us in truth. It could only ever hold us in truth. We are made of silence, we come from silence, and in the end, we return to silence—and throughout it all, silence is our indestructible and immortal core of truth.

Deeper still, silence is the gateway to the Divine Beloved. It is the deep and infinite chamber within where the Beloved rests, breathing deeply, inhaling life, exhaling death. In every cell of this divine breath, the cycles and seasons of all of life are held and emanate. In every moment, a lifetime. In each breath, the universe. This stillness is the nucleus of our being and the truth within our every cell.

Meeting with Silence

To meet the true Self and the heaven within, we must first meet silence—for everything that takes us to truth arrives there through silence. When we are still lost in the gobble of the world, the meeting cannot happen. It is too precious, too quiet. It can only happen in the absolute stillness of our being.

Ultimately, it is indeed the door of silence that opens to God, although there are many doors and many ways that can lead us to this door of silence. We can dance into silence. We can sing into silence. We can commune with nature into silence. We can cry into silence. We can stretch into silence. We can run or shower or chant into silence. Ultimately, the one thing we must know is this: the gateway of silence will carry us home.

Within silence is total freedom. We could even say it like this: freedom is made of silence. It is the space from which we are able to hear and recognize truth and, therefore, respond to the calls of life, the ones that beckon us into supernatural alignment. Silence is the only telephone line through which we can clearly hear the messages from the Divine in all its forms—the smile of a stranger, the whispers of the trees, the song that just synchronistically popped up on your iPod—somehow answering a deep question of yours.

Does silence mean there are no thoughts or no mind? No. It could mean that, but it is not necessary. Being within the silence means you are still, unmoving, meditative, and that even with whatever is happening in your life, and even when there are rounds of wild thoughts stampeding through your mind, you are consciously connected to that timeless, eternal, wordless space within. Being within the silence means you are allowing yourself to observe and experience life from the seat of the witness, as the witness itself.

The seat of the witness is carved from silence. For the seat of the witness to deepen and stabilize, the space of silence must be practiced, and it must become our anchor. It is our daily practice of orienting and reorienting with silence that allows our silent presence to anchor. And although silence is the most natural state of our being, modern life is not only out of sync with this quietness, but it is also opposed to it. Therefore, our practice of meditation is crucial so that we may hold our true vibration in a world that may otherwise influence us out of it. Indeed, our commitment to meditation is a vehicle to our remembering, and the ceremony of life is an ongoing meditation.

Root in Silence

Silence is unity. When you root firmly in unity and experience duality from there, you remain consciously connected to the great space within where expansion and love take place, and this connection greatly changes the experience of life. Indeed, you may experience all the tears, all the waves that may come, all the different moments of life from the same point of view: the point of view of your Self. Then there is no need, no temptation, and no attraction to slip into any deluding solutions of transcending duality and denying the gorgeous earthly experiences, because you are already allowing yourself to rest in that great and ultimate love. Because you are already safe. Then there is no need to be so split in your life. First, be one with your Self and then, and only then, can you welcome in the madness of life with a happy, stable spirit. Then you can dance in the eye of the storm, laughing madly, seeing clearly, savoring the strange and delightful feeling of the rain upon your precious human skin.

Then you can burn your umbrellas, your white robes, and your mantras and just peel the potatoes. Then you can feel your heart being tickled when the mantra reappears, singing from your soul, immortal, rising again, fresh and light in a new moment of life. Then you can really be grateful to your dog for his friendship, to the rain for watering our precious earth, for the tears that fall from your eyes, honoring your passing feelings and releasing energy ready to be transformed. To delight in the starry mud of this beautiful human experience from the infinitely grateful space of God, to be turned on by the morning light, the squeaking of chairs in group meditation, the sound of the plates crashing when the waiter drops his tray—now that, that is the good stuff. That is where it's at.

When we root out in the place of oneness and experience life from there, the highs and lows and the trials and tribulations of life are experienced with a certain grace, and our hearts expand. Rather than being in our ego-based reactions, we find ourselves in just the right position for this particular divine alchemy to work and to grace our lives with our heartfelt responses. Our rooting in the silence of unity consciousness allows our very hearts to expand within the inclusive experience of duality. And this is mastery. This is the gift of the Self. This is the juice.

Chapter 18

OPENING INTO ACCEPTANCE

> Clearly recognizing what is happening inside us, and regarding
> what we see with an open, kind and loving heart, is what I call
> Radical Acceptance. If we are holding back from any part of our
> experience, if our heart shuts out any part of who we are and
> what we feel, we are fueling the fears and feelings of separation
> that sustain the trance of unworthiness. Radical Acceptance
> directly dismantles the very foundations of this trance.
>
> TARA BRACH, *Radical Acceptance*

When we open into acceptance we move into wholeness, and for that we become able to receive and enliven that which the moment has for us. Once the message or offering has been sensed through our reverent, silent listening, we have the opportunity to say yes to it through our accepting nature. We accept when we simply *do not resist* and drop more and more into openness with that which is both within us and before us. Because our receptivity is dependent upon our willingness to accept, acceptance is necessary for our ongoing discovery of meaning. By choosing to accept what is happening and what is being offered, our adventure with the moment begins.

When we orient toward acceptance, we place the stethoscope of awareness upon our heart to make sure it is opening. Then we place it upon our general being to see if any resistance is directing the show. We check to make sure we are breathing good and deep. Any contraction we find, we breathe into, and we open endlessly wider, knowing life can never hurt us—only our perception of it can.

To help bring it more to life, imagine acceptance as forgiveness manifest. It is forgiveness for this moment, for the past, for yourself, for all the pain and sorrow that ever held you. When you truly accept, you have forgiven, and that very forgiveness washes away that which needed cleansing as a simple consequence of your acceptance. Acceptance is an openness toward ourselves and to this moment so total that within it is our absolution. And within acceptance is surrender, which we will get to soon. These are universes within universes, the very cosmic stuff we are made of.

When we accept, we are present, and when we are present, we accept. The two are shimmers of the same light and live together as intrinsic frequencies of truth. Our acceptance of everything this moment holds brings us back to the now. The gift of being is that we *are* the moment. And so we always are able to enter the present moment so totally and completely, to the point of merging and union, for after all, we are that.

The gift of this union, in coming to the present moment so completely, is that within it, the pains of the past dissolve and dissipate, as they are neither here nor now, and therefore they can only be phenomenal, mortal, and gone. Their seeming presence in the moment comes from the memory, and that memory's seeming presence is nothing more than an imprint. All that is true is eternal and always present. And this whole alchemy can wash us so deeply that it can penetrate and reprieve all layers and levels of our soul. Through these moments our divine memory rises to the surface. Through these moments—the moments home.

As mentioned in earlier chapters, the pain we are still resolving can be present with us, and indeed, it deserves our attention, love, and care. What we're focusing on here is the deeply restorative nature of acceptance and presence. Presence is healing. To be present is to heal your perspective—to heal your perspective out of the past, out of the future, out of time, out of isolation, and into this moment and the divine, eternal nature of your being. It is to align your focus back with that which is happening now, that which is real right now. Acceptance and forgiveness are forever found unwavering within you, within the present moment.

The footpath home is made of forgiveness, and the acceptance of your being allows you to move forward upon it. Through forgiveness, you get closer to remembering your innate freedom. Through acceptance, you enter the wave of alignment that delivers your true Self. It can deliver you to the door of silence, and through the door of silence is enough love to create a billion worlds.

There is great freedom in realizing this very forgiveness is actually just our effortless, natural pulse. This is true forgiveness, and it begins with ourselves. When we forgive ourselves, we forgive everyone else, too, for our forgiveness of others is simply a reflection of our own union and integration with our forgiving nature.

Scripted forgiveness and intellectual forgiveness toward ourselves and others are empty. Stopping there only prevents us from dropping into the deep and true forgiveness and acceptance we are discussing here. Our very essence is acceptance of all of life itself, including all that has happened and all that will come to be. It's an embodiment of the wisdom that *there is no right or wrong; there simply is.* There is no resistance; there is only allowing. There is only freedom.

Acceptance and Free Will

Acceptance does not mean you take whatever is coming to you in the external world lying down, with no questions, in blind faith. When we talk about divine acceptance, we are talking about the general flow of life, the surprises that catch us, the inner mystery, the transitions and unexpected turns. We are talking about the energy of life and our dialogue with life on a moment-to-moment basis. We are talking about acceptance of that which is for our best and highest good, and having the humility to know we do not always know the way there or what will change throughout the ceremony of it all.

When all is forgiven, nothing is left, and only freedom remains. You have forgiven your parents, and so their voices disappear from the house. You have forgiven your past, and so all the knickknacks and picture frames of what once was vanish from the counters and walls. You have forgiven the foundation of the house for its shortcomings, and so it, too, disappears. And the attic and the roof, the pieces of broken mugs, and anything else that might be left dematerialize until you are standing there alone and naked, just you and the breeze, realizing you were only ever this free. Realizing you were never actually held captive by anything at all.

You have let go of the past and the future. Liberated from the illusions of time, you realize you are able to be present. And then, the more present you are, the more you realize being present is not something you are or are not able to do; it is simply what you are—the witness of your life, the present awareness that is always here, now. Accepting, witnessing, breathing, being.

The very existence of acceptance is forever, for it is an aspect of God and an indigenous element of creation. It is the aspect that does not resist and therefore allows, whose very allowance permits movement and therefore permits reception, creation, and evolution. Acceptance is part of the immortal rhythm of life, the universe, and the Divine.

Acceptance is the most natural whisper of your being, the most natural temperament of your heart, and the most natural rhythm of your breath. Its gift to you is that it allows the ceremony of your life to move along. And it waits for nothing but your divine give-up, for within that you will realize you did not create acceptance, but rather fell into that which already was—that which waited for you like a bed of clouds, infinitely soft, kind, and there.

Chapter 19

RELEASING INTO SURRENDER

> I used to have a sign pinned up on my wall that read: "Only to
> the extent that we expose ourselves over and over to annihilation
> can that which is indestructible in us be found in us."
>
> PEMA CHÖDRÖN, *When Things Fall Apart*

Once we are in acceptance we may be taken by the current of
surrender. Surrender follows our acceptance. First, we accept
what is happening, which sets into motion the energy of both
the seen and unseen worlds of the present moment, and then,
when we give ourselves over to that energy of divine flow to have
our way with us, we are surrendered, we are within the motion.
Through that process not only may we meet that which is absolute within us, but we also discover that which the universe has
in store for us. Surrender is the flow of the river, and only when
we let that river take us will we begin to know its gifts.

Choosing to drop into surrender in the most challenging
moments of the ceremony of life—the ones when we are
certain that if we go any further, we will either die or fall
apart—is crucial. In these moments, the flow of surrender is
what will pull us into the transformation we need if we are
to be more free, more open, more integrated as the Self, and

more receptive and giving of love. As we open into acceptance, we can tune in a bit deeper to sense if we are really giving ourselves over to the energy of the moment, for *that* is surrender. It is not anything that can be done; rather, it is absolute relinquishment and being taken.

To put it more poetically, within the depth of acceptance, a cosmic river can be felt pulsing, pulling, pushing, and carrying us along our way. This river is always pulling us into deeper alignment and harmony. It moves only by the grace of God, infinitely taking us to that which is most aligned for us.

Surrender is letting yourself be played like a flute of God. The breath of God, filled with vision, moves through the channel of your being and therefore moves your Self. All of life around you moves in response to your song. And you are taken.

There is only yes, there is only now. There is only a divine release of effort, of opinion, of personalized will. There is only a giving it back to God. This is the ultimate current of trust, where we throw our selves into the water to die, to be taken, and to know our true Self more and more. Where we give ourselves over to simply be taken through the moments. No glorified words or hopes. Simply trusting, simply being taken to where is next. Knowing that wherever is next is "best," for it *is*, and so it is *given* to us, it is our ceremony, and it is sacred.

We must also allow ourselves to surrender to the "good" things in life. Surrender to happiness, to love, to a crazy fit of laughter. Pain is, indeed, not the only thing we resist. We are often afraid of joy and love because it can feel so much more familiar, safe, and comfortable to be constricted, alone, in our painful patterns, and so on. Love, laughter, joy—they all open us, and they all push us to open up more. To be in love—to *be love*—is to be vulnerable and open, again and again.

Fuck It

When in resistance or challenge, often to "just surrender" can feel impossible and like the most obnoxious suggestion. This is a moment of perceived dilemma, and in this moment you might be best off saying "Fuck it" to surrendering—and to everything, for that matter. With effort and too much pressure, the simplicity of letting go can become riddled into concept, rather than into opening into the heart.

We're all very familiar with what *fuck it* means. We can forget about it all just as easily as we can snap our fingers. And actually, saying "Fuck it" is a form of surrender. When we say *fuck it* in moments of resistance or challenge, we are on our way to surrendering. *Fuck it* gives us space, reminds us to not take things too seriously, and gives us a permission to chill that we may deeply need. So sometimes, the *fuck it* can save us, too. Let it. We all know it's a good way to cope and also to enjoy.

Surrender, *fuck it*—whatever takes you there, let it take you. Sometimes your *fuck it* is a glass of wine, a candlelit bath, an episode of *Seinfeld*, an intense workout, or a walk in the woods. Whatever it is, your *fuck it* is good so long as it helps you naturally relax and release in a way that supports your peace. This isn't the *fuck it* that evades accountability, but the one that honors the space and relaxation you need to become ready for that accountability. Anything that helps you to relax is taking you toward surrender, the truth within, and your freedom. Speeding down the highway, amazed by the gorgeous sky, you feel the inherent freedom of life, a certain song comes on the radio—and something changes.

It must be remembered that the cosmic hand is not always gentle, and it is not meant to be. For sure, it is intense, strong, and spookily direct at times. If you work with it wisely, it will always help you make changes in your life and break down the necessary barriers to open you into freedom. Make no mistake about it, this divine cosmic blow will come and come again when it needs to, whether you are resisting or surrendered. But when you *are* aware of your surrender, melting *into* it and *becoming* it, the blows and twists, the laughter, joy, and pain are all experienced differently. They're all given in to, and in the process you are chiseled and shaped by the wisdom, depth, and grace that become unearthed within you. In this way, surrender takes you again and again to know the depth of your divine knowingness, the expanse of your freedom, and the possibilities therein.

DISAPPEARING INTO CELEBRATION

Old pond
frog jumps in—
splash.

BASHŌ, in *The Enlightened Heart* (Stephen Mitchell, editor)

Celebration is the miraculous movement of life. It's an invitation to take life less seriously, to remain as the childlike masters we inherently are, playing wildly with life, expressing ourselves freely from the heart, and loving all that comes. This is our birthright; this is the song of our hearts. Celebrating isn't always fanfare and trumpets, although it can be. And it isn't all ecstasy and bliss either, although it can be those, too. Celebration is simply the percolation that happens as we realize the miracles that are before us. Everything is worth celebrating simply because it is, and simply that *it is* is miraculous. In any given moment, we have the opportunity to check in to see if we are celebrating the moment, no matter how mundane, challenging, or simple it may seem.

Celebration is the beauty mark of freedom. Freedom is another word for love. And really, what else is there to do but celebrate love?

Everything that we do as an outpouring of love is celebration, be it working, writing, singing, washing the dishes, or raising our children. The golden nugget of love within everything we witness and do is the source of celebration. When we nurture this golden nugget, the outpouring of love amplifies and can be felt, and so that which we do becomes a celebration.

As we begin to realize how precious life is, and how precious the breath of life is, the way of our lives becomes more obviously sacred. We have more care for the steps we take, more respect for the moments that arise, and we realize that to kneel before life with our hands cupped to the sky is to save our lives.

Hands raised, cupped to the sky, we offer up our hearts, we offer up our Selves, to be saved and filled by the breath of God. We say, "I am so totally alone, and I can't do this alone. So enter me so I can see how loved I am, how I am love itself, and how I can only ever really be One." This is the way of offering yourself up to be celebrated by existence. This is the dance of freedom.

When we realize how deep this love is within us, everything becomes a celebration. Life itself becomes the celebration. The tears, the sweat, the glasses crashing, the dog barking—all can be felt as love manifest. All can be noticed for the God-love pulse within, and then, what else is there to do but be tantalized by the miracle of life and discover how that miracle moves us?

Births, sex, breakups, funerals, leaving a job, falling asleep each night, waking each morning, putting on our clothes, pouring a cup of coffee—all becomes sacred ceremony. All is realized for its sacred nature, its sacred gift, its sacred treasure. All is appreciated and marveled at in wonderment of its miraculous nature and the magic it holds within. This is the alchemy that takes us home.

In this moment, the only thing to do is breathe deeply and gently, courageous and vulnerable at the doorstep of God. We are always at the doorstep of God. Nothing else is possible. Simply by existing we are simultaneously at the doorstep of God and God itself. We are the Creator and the Created. The Created sees itself as split until it remembers its source. And for as long as we see ourselves as isolated and split, we perceive ourselves as separate from God, and so we are at the doorstep of God. But we can never be anywhere else—only at the doorstep of God, waiting to remember our Self, or remembering our Self as the heart of God itself. We can only be at the doorstep or walking through the door over and over again in all of the gorgeous ways we can.

Human as we are, we find ourselves at the doorstep time and time again as we grow through these human conditions. The conditions we may perceive ourselves as trapped in always give way to freedom, for we are caught within them *in* freedom. As it's been stated here in various ways, we have allowed ourselves to feel trapped in order to evolve and learn through the paradox of life.

The heart's very pulse is a pulse that opens. It beats. It is the drumbeat of our beings, gently caressing and relaxing our body into welcoming the expansive energy of our more opened heart. This drumbeat softens us, coaxes us into allowing the opening. It prepares us. *Beat. Beat. Beat. Boom. Boom. Boom.* Faster and faster it goes when the nerves strike up. *Open. Open. Open. Open to save your life. Relax to save your life.* We know this, our bodies know this: we must give ourselves the permission to remember, the permission to trust our inner knowings.

Give yourself that permission now.

Celebration is the sparkle in the eye of the one who glows. It is the song that plays in the house of freedom. Celebration is the dance of life. It's the one dancing to the drumbeat of the heart. It's your birthday cake. It's you blowing out the trick candles. It's you delighting in the fire of life.

Where there is freedom, there is love, there is peace. And then, tell me, what is there *not* to celebrate? That fuzzy radio static, the layers of snow that have piled on the car, the absolute miracle of french fries, Orion's Belt, children's laughter—everything holds within it the gorgeous spark of God. And when it's reflected back to you, all there's left to do is smile.

Permission to Celebrate

Celebration is the way we most naturally move. We must recognize that so much of this world is dependent upon our lack of celebration. Too happy a society means less work and less money. We are groomed to live an uncelebratory life—one where celebrations are limited to designated dates and events. We have been conditioned to be "normal" and not laugh too much at unnecessary things. We have been molded to be controlled and tame. It is now time to reignite our wildness and reclaim what is ours.

Life is a celebration. A happy heart celebrates the embrace of a friend, morning coffee, and even sadness. A happy heart celebrates the opportunity to grow. Beneath all layers of declared unhappiness is the happiness itself, and behind all ideas of what happiness is rests contentment, the peacefulness that we are that is never changing and never circumstantial. Indeed, the heart is love and contentedness manifest, and it says that whatever is, is enough and is worth celebrating, even if only very quietly.

Celebrate more, and you will see that life is worth celebrating. Osho said that the quickest path to enlightenment is celebration, and I love that. Dance, move your body, and through your celebration and your dancing energy will shift; stuck energy will move; and you will transform. You give yourself back to the source that you are a part of—you give it all back to God—and miracles just keep happening. You get over your*self* and into your true Self. The ideas you have about yourself, no matter how awesome, are nothing more than decorated, fake-jewel-encrusted barriers to the greatest joys.

You need no reason to celebrate. Only the mind needs reason; the soul never does. You do not need to celebrate a "happy" thing. Just get up and give yourself over to the mystery; let your body be moved by the divine breath that flows through you, and you will be shown the celebration. You will be shown the ceremony.

Grace falls upon us when we least expect it. We are washing the dishes in the sink, and we become deeply aware of the way the water feels on our skin. We are peaceful in this present moment of nothing but this cleaning of the dishes. We observe and savor the shape of the dish, the water turning off, the sound of the dish being placed upon the drying rack, and throughout, we are touched by this grace of witnessing. We let ourselves be cleansed with the dishes, washed by the totality of the moment. A formerly mundane moment is restored to the sacred moment it truly is, and we, with life, we are celebrating. With our breath, we're breathing in God; we're breathing out moments passed, the stars in the night—and the eternal sparkles shine, and we're celebrating. And the once *mundane* becomes the *miraculous mundane* once again.

And we realize life is one big song, one continuous ceremony. We realize the beingness that is eternal, and that the very course of beingness, the very moments of beingness, are miraculous and precious and glints of one infinite stream. The ceremony is life itself, one never-ending ceremony within the great big ceremony. We realize the very meaning of this sacred walk of life could only ever be life itself—and that all of this could only ever be divine life, dripping from the fingertips of God, reflected back to us as the life we see.

Chapter 21

A CEREMONY
CALLED LIFE

Before Zen, mountains were mountains and trees were trees. During Zen, mountains were thrones of the spirits and trees were the voices of wisdom. After Zen, mountains were mountains and trees were trees.

OLD BUDDHIST PROVERB

No matter where we are along our journey, we are in a moment of the ceremony of life. As the proverb above suggests, as we mature spiritually, we realize that what we once regarded as mundane is actually the very most beautiful thing in the world. Indeed, that such sacred beauty is normal and that it comprises the daily stuff of our lives is the simple and profound nature of things that we get to exist within every day. Letting life be the meaning of life itself is what it means to live life as ceremony, for in that sacred undoing, every moment is revolutionary and evolutionary.

The portrait of this ceremonial life is imbued with the knowing that every moment is either teaching us something or offering itself up for our enjoyment. And somehow, without knowing why, we know that this way of living is the deep drink of life. In this way, the sacred offering of life becomes more and more apparent and more and more clear. It comes to life right before our very eyes, and what we realize is *it was always there*. Perhaps we missed it before, but not again.

In the seed of every living being and every living thing is the creative principle—*our divine essence*—and we both *live* and *live out* this divine essence in the gel of a timeless world. We *live* it because we are it. We *live it out* because we project it from within to create our lives. We are Creator and Created, the two that can only be One, walking our life, singing our song, drunk off the stars, crying over a lover, falling off the horse and getting back on.

And we sing and sing the refrain of this song, vocals on the rise, voice shaky with rawness and conviction: *imperfection is our gift*. To see where we slip is a gift, for it allows us to excavate and go deeper than we ever had before. We are alive because we are changing and growing and transforming all the time, and thank God for that. Thank God for the imperfect choices we make, for they are a part of the journey, and it is the journey itself that brings us into the state of empowerment we desire and we know to be true.

Whatever happens is a part of our lives, and by virtue of that simple qualification, it is good. It is fine, it is enough, it simply is. Moments of triumph are just as precious as getting lost on the road, for both are precisely what get us home in the right moment. It can be too easy to miss in a world where our orientation is so far removed from the sacredness of every moment, and yet it is definitive: every moment is an opportunity, an invitation home.

Every moment offers itself to us as a blank canvas, and upon it we have the pristine privilege to project whatever we are holding inside. Aware of this, we remain sharp and more sharp to gift ourselves the life we know is possible: we project from our heart the simple present love of our being. When there is a vision that arrives in divine ways or as a surprise within our heart, we project and share that, too. And we trust in life to take us where we need to be even when we cannot see the way or recognize the steps. We tune back in relentlessly again and again to make sure we are seeing ourselves and our lives the way God is.

We meditate. We meditate every day until life itself becomes the meditation. We recognize the gift of the cherry blossoms to be a reminder from God of the impermanence of all things, for after two weeks, they are gone. We watch the seasons cycle and come and go and the snake shed his skin; we watch the phase of the moon change. We watch the stars fall and the clouds collide into storms, and, miraculously still, we watch a new day be born in clearness and sunshine and calm.

We let the universal truths of nature and of life permeate our beings and enchant our souls until we breathe them in with every breath we take. Until every cup of tea is the ultimate tea of life, replete with wisdom, teeming with the love of a million gods, infused with our prayer. And we drink in the creation of our lives.

In moments of darkness, confusion, and destitution, we give ourselves over. We enter into the divine give-up for life to take us, to forget it all and to die, to be demolished, to be turned into dust and reborn. And we beat on. Reborn after tragedy, we drink a Cherry Coke and watch the beaten flag wave in the wind. Ragged and worn it is, but it is upon the pole again and waving. It is ready once more.

A new dawn heralds, life begins anew, spring comes, and you cry upon the grass the tears of heaven, thrown into a gratitude beyond you, blown open into the mystery of this life, at her heels merciless and kissing the ground. Now, again, a newness in your steps. "Thank you, Earth, for holding these feet as they walk. Thank you for having me," you say in silence. Your whole being vibrates at the frequency of the sun itself and the brilliant light of universes untold—the universes untold of your heart. And your curiosity, humility, and love of it all lead the way.

Silence is born unto you. A home in the high mountains of Tibet still does not feel right, for your heart still comes alive at the sound of the city streets. And so, alone in your home, comfortable with a good book, interruption comes. The phone rings. It is a trivial matter, and you are upset, but you laugh. You laugh silently at yourself for your humanity. You laugh with your humanity itself. You laugh at the absurdity of it all. "What can I do," you ask, "but be me? What more can I do? What more can I give?"

On and on it goes. You explore your brilliance through another day. Or your sorrow. Or your enchantment. And in the twilight of the days of null, you watch, you wait, you listen. Within your inner gaze, you laugh with, wait—who is that? Yourself? God? You laugh with the cosmic presence at the marvel that life ever came to be, that here you are, sitting amongst it, knowing less than you ever did, and infinitely richer. And you begin.

ACKNOWLEDGMENTS

Thank you to my love, Carl, for so much and so many things related to this writing and not related to this writing, and all of which are one and the same, a thank-you that can simply be said as . . . thank you for your love, and the beautiful way that you love.

Thank you to my mother/soul sister for always supporting me, cheering me on, and believing in me. I call in the dragonflies and insert a space of silence here to acknowledge the profound way you have supported me throughout my life, always. To my father, thank you for encouraging my creativity, independence, freedom, and my knowingness of my "worth." It is a beautiful thing to write a thank-you to you both, side by side.

To my sisters, Catrine, Adya, Aya, and Tammy, thank you for holding the prayer of this book in your hearts while it was still marinating in the stars, and thank you for sharing with me in the wild magic of womanhood and sisterhood. Thank you also to loves Liz, Erin, and Jessie, who were so present and nurturing during the birthing of the book. Sisters, thank you all for sharing your gorgeousness with me; you inspire me in so many ways, and I am so happy that you live in my heart.

Also in the realm of friendship, thank you to Scott for always being curious and enthusiastic about whatever creativity has come out of me over the years. Years ago, you were my first friend to be interested and excited about my writings—you gave me a loving space to share—and that has meant the world to me.

Thank you, Devra Jacobs, my psychic agent, for partaking in the magic of our meeting and for believing in me. Thank you also to Dr. Carmen Harra, who was a major weaver of the landing of this book into reality.

Thank you to Amy Rost, godmother of the book, for an editorial prowess that is truly amazing. The weaving of your intelligence, intuition, and precision has been a tremendous blessing to this work. I can't thank you enough.

Thank you to Jennifer Brown and Brian Galvin for being so open to my writing and for receiving it with such excitement, kindness, and appreciation. Thank you also to Tami Simon and the rest of the Sounds True family for believing in me and taking a chance on an unknown writer, and for all of the gentle support you have given both me and the book. It is an honor to be in such good company and to feel the care of such a wonderful publishing house.

To Kristie Reeves, healing facilitator and friend, our work together helped me to open and commit to writing, sharing, and more. Thank you for your continued support over the years—I am blessed to know you and to get to work with you. (For anyone interested in learning more about Kristie, visit kristiereeves.com.)

Thank you also to Urte Huset, a café in Copenhagen, for your delicious sandwiches and treats that sustained me while I wrote this book at your tables day after day.

Pachamama, thank you for holding me as my heart broke enough to finally open, for teaching me what it means to celebrate, and for introducing me to the magic of these good Earth ways. Thank you for so much more. The prayer of this book blossomed while with you.

These acknowledgments would not be complete without a thank-you to the copious amounts of tea and chocolate consumed whilst editing that no doubt became part of both my blood and the book. And to the redwoods, hummingbirds, deer, vultures, hawks, bees, butterflies, and the countless tiny birds and other creatures that play in our backyard, reflecting to me the goodness of life every day. And to the water that kept me hydrated, clean, and fluid; the fire that kept me focused and firm; the wind that kept wiping me clean and carrying the seeds of the prayer to their best, most fertile ground. To the earth that gave the prayer roots. To the sun that keeps inspiring all the life, and the moon that patiently watched on, cycling it all through its seasons, holding it all in glowing radiant wisdom. To the mysterious divinity that continues to guide the way. You know, *to life*.

To the readers, thank you for welcoming this book into your hearts and opening yourselves to be touched. It is amazing the large and small ways we can share in each other's journeys, and I am deeply grateful for your presence in mine.

ABOUT THE AUTHOR

Tehya Sky (who goes by her birth name, Sky) walked away from a successful career in the music industry to dedicate herself to inner work and helping others find greater meaning in life. Today, she is a metaphysical guide and writer who offers workshops internationally.

Having been naturally attuned to the power we have in creating our lives since she was a child, Sky was suspicious of the complacency and dissatisfaction that once saturated her life. Determined to break out of the dysfunctional conditions that shaped her, she went through a deep transformation and now shares the wisdom that awakened inside of her. Her daily practice is infused with tantric meditation, deep breathing, lots of tea and chocolate, and remaining present through whatever shows up in life. Her greatest and oldest teachers are poetry, nature, and the light. Sky also writes poetry, inspired by the boundless depths of this divine life. For more, please visit tehyasky.com.

ABOUT SOUNDS TRUE

Sounds True is a multimedia publisher whose mission is to inspire and support personal transformation and spiritual awakening. Founded in 1985 and located in Boulder, Colorado, we work with many of the leading spiritual teachers, thinkers, healers, and visionary artists of our time. We strive with every title to preserve the essential "living wisdom" of the author or artist. It is our goal to create products that not only provide information to a reader or listener, but that also embody the quality of a wisdom transmission.

For those seeking genuine transformation, Sounds True is your trusted partner. At SoundsTrue.com you will find a wealth of free resources to support your journey, including exclusive weekly audio interviews, free downloads, interactive learning tools, and other special savings on all our titles.

To learn more, please visit SoundsTrue.com/freegifts or call us toll-free at 800.333.9185.